To Jonathan

Best Wishes

The
Final Score

The
Final Score

The Inside Story
of Soccer's Trial
of the Century

Hans Segers,
Mel Goldberg
and Alan Thatcher

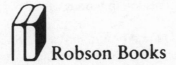

Robson Books

First published in Great Britain in 1998 by Robson Books Ltd,
Bolsover House, 5-6 Clipstone Street, London W1P 8LE

British Library Cataloguing in Publication Data
A catalogue record for this title is available from the British Library

ISBN 1 86105 106 9

Printed and bound in Great Britain by
WBC Limited, Bridgend.

To Astrid, Brigitte, Nicky,
Gay, James and Laura

Alexander, Richard and Nova;
Sunshine, happiness and laughter,
Be yours now and forever after

CONTENTS

ACKNOWLEDGEMENTS

When you come to write a book like this, there is a natural reflection that takes hold of your life. I would like to dedicate my book to those people who have influenced me most and supported me through bad times and good. Without their help I would not have reached this stage in my life.

Thank you to Mark McGhee, manager of Wolverhampton Wanderers Football Cub, and all their supporters for showing faith in me.

To Desmond de Silva, a mighty man; Stephen Berrick, Mel Goldberg, Jan Cook and the team at Epstein, Grower and Michael Freeman for their legal excellence.

To Alan Thatcher and the editor and staff of Robson Books.

Thank you to Church Crookham Baptist Church and all my Christian brothers and sisters who have supported me, particularly with prayer.

To Bob Wilson, a true professional; and to Imran Khan, for his help during the trials.

Thank you to the members of the jury, who, having listened to the evidence, produced a fair and just result.

To my friends, Dennis Kelly and Neil Stringer. Thank you to all the people who helped with babysitting and childminding for their care and support.

Special thanks to Graham and Lynda Smith for being there all the time, for their prayers and love, and for Graham's help with this book.

My special thanks to my lovely wife, Astrid, for her undying love and support and my two great kids, Brigitte and Nicky, who mean the world to me.

And finally to the Lord Jesus Christ, to whom I owe my life. I praise and thank you for your gift.

Hans Segers

INTRODUCTION

By Alan Thatcher

Waiting for the verdict seemed to take an eternity.

For three professional footballers, used to an all-action lifestyle, it was hard to sit still outside the court and wait for the jury to deliver its result on soccer's match-fixing trial.

The players, Hans Segers, Bruce Grobbelaar and John Fashanu, were used to playing in front of big crowds at football's major venues. Here, the drama was being enacted in the cramped confines of a courtroom in the historic and genteel Hampshire county town of Winchester.

In footballing terms, they were waiting for the penalties to begin after extra time in the replay. The first trial, which had begun eight months earlier, had ended in a no-score draw after the jury failed to reach a verdict.

Action in the replay trial followed an almost identical pattern as the defendants' footballing careers, private lives, social lives and part-time business activities were once again exposed to the world.

Segers, Grobbelaar and Fashanu had been charged, along with Malaysian businessman Richard Lim, with attempting to rig the outcome of English Premiership matches so that Far Eastern gambling syndicates could win huge sums of money by betting on the results. The outcome of the case hinged largely on how much credence the jury placed on a 'sting' operation involving *The Sun* newspaper and Zimbabwean businessman Chris Vincent. He was a former business partner of Grobbelaar's who had turned against his friend when the Mondoro game reserve venture they were organizing in Zimbabwe had run into difficulties.

It took two trials, millions of pounds of taxpayers' money, and two and a half years out of the three footballers' lives before the verdicts were delivered.

The case, named Operation Navaho by Hampshire Police, began

with a series of dawn raids that led to the arrests of the central characters alleged to be involved.

The result of the trial had huge implications for the multi-million pound football industry. After all, who would want to pay inflated prices for admission to soccer's new, all-seated luxury stadia if they thought the outcome of the match had been fixed in advance? As a result, the trial attracted enormous media coverage around the world, especially with so many famous names either in the dock or in the witness box. Football itself was on trial.

At the time of the police investigations, more than 200 players, referees and officials connected with Malaysian football had been sent to prison for their involvement in a massive match-fixing ring. The assumption was that, as the Malaysian authorities had cleaned up football in their own country, the organized gambling syndicates had been forced to look elsewhere and had targeted the English Premiership. This, of course, was denied.

The prosecution alleged that Johannes Josef and an associate, Loe Bon Sue, were leaders of a gambling syndicate based in Indonesia who employed Lim as a middle man, to send back information about forthcoming matches. It also alleged that one of Lim's primary functions was to recruit players such as Fashanu, Grobbelaar and Segers to help influence the results of matches. Again, these charges were vigorously denied by the accused.

Police monitored a visit to London by Josef and Bon Sue, where calls were traced between them and Lim, and to Fashanu, using the name Buckle, and from Fashanu and Lim to Segers and Grobbelaar. Josef and Bon Sue were known to be wealthy and enthusiastic gamblers. Police investigations into allegations of match-fixing also led them to Australia and Africa.

It was not the first time a scandal involving gambling allegations had rocked English football. Back in the 1960s a trio of players from Sheffield Wednesday, Peter Swan, Tony Kaye and Bronco Lane, had pleaded guilty to rigging the results of matches and were sent to prison. The sums of money involved were peanuts compared to the amounts of cash alleged to be changing hands among Lim, Fashanu, Segers and Grobbelaar.

Elsewhere, the European soccer authorities, UEFA, investigated claims that a Romanian referee was bribed before a European Cup Winners' Cup tie involving Porto and Aberdeen in 1984 and Anderlecht and Nottingham Forest in the same year. In Russia, several major clubs are feared to have come under the control of the Moscow mafia. In Colombia, a drugs cartel had heavily backed the national team to beat the host nation America in the 1994 World Cup finals. However, an own goal by defender Andres Escobar contributed to a shock 2-1 defeat in the Pasadena Rose Bowl. When he returned to his home town of Medellin, Colombia's cocaine capital, Escobar was shot dead by a gunman following an argument outside a nightclub when angry supporters criticized his performance. It was the ultimate sporting sacrifice, providing a tragic twist to the saying attributed to former Liverpool manager Bill Shankly: 'Football's not a matter of life and death, it's much more important than that.'

Major Colombian clubs are believed to be controlled by powerful drug barons and the country was briefly suspended from international football after six armed men demanded that a referee ensure victory for Atletico Nacional against a Brazilian team in Medellin in September 1990. An earlier president of Medellin, Pablo Escobar (no relation), was extradited to the US in 1984 on drug money laundering charges. International player Leonel Alvarez was photographed visiting Escobar in prison. Controversial goalkeeper Rene Higuita, who captivated a Wembley crowd with his famous overhead 'scorpion' kick, was dropped from the international team in 1996 after being jailed following charges that he had profited from a kidnapping.

Former French politician Bernard Tapie, the owner of Olympique Marseille and Adidas, was jailed for attempting to rig the result of a French League match one week before Marseille were due to face AC Milan in the 1993 final of the European Cup. Tapie had instructed the club's general manager, Jean-Pierre Bernes, to approach players from Valenciennes and offer them £30,000 each to 'take it easy', so that no Marseille players were injured. Two years earlier Marseille had lost the European Cup final to Red Star

Belgrade after several key players picked up injuries. This time Tapie was determined to have a full-strength team available to face Milan, owned by Silvio Berlusconi, the Italian television mogul of whom Tapie was believed to be immensely envious. The ploy worked and Marseille won the final 1-0.

But Tapie's activities were about to be exposed. Valenciennes players admitted to receiving offers, but claimed they had changed their minds before taking the field. In the trial that followed, Tapie denied all the accusations until Bernes suddenly appeared as chief witness for the prosecution. Tapie was found guilty and received an eight-month prison sentence. Later, he was also convicted of embezzling club funds and sentenced to a further 18 months in jail, with another 18 months suspended.

At one time Tapie had been a French government minister and was one of the most popular figures in France. But his empire came crashing down as a web of fraud and deceit was exposed. As we put the finishing touches to this book, former Italian Premier Berlusconi also received a prison sentence for corruption associated with his political activities. He may never see the inside of a cell. He enjoys parliamentary immunity and has the right to two appeals.

One of the greatest names in Italian football, the striker Paolo Rossi, had been banned for three years in 1980 for his involvement in a match-fixing scandal. That sentence was cynically reduced to two years to allow him to play in the 1982 World Cup – and he then scored six goals as Italy won the trophy in Spain. Ten other players had originally been arrested and thrown into jail in Rome, but no charges were brought against any of those involved because the Italians 'discovered' that sporting fraud was not a criminal offence.

In England, several individuals have been accused of corruption in transfer deals, with managers, coaches and agents allegedly involved in offering and accepting inducements, more commonly known as bungs, to help deals go through. The chairman of Tottenham Hotspur, Sugar, went on record as saying that he was horrified by many of the customs and practices surrounding

English football clubs, especially those concerning transfer negotiations.

Despite a massive investigation by the Football Association and the Inland Revenue, George Graham is the only manager to have been punished, sacked by Arsenal and banned from football for a year following the acceptance of an unsolicited gift from the Norwegian agent Rune Hauge. Charges were laid against former Nottingham Forest manager Brian Clough, who was alleged to have asked for £50,000 during the transfer of Teddy Sheringham from Nottingham Forest to Tottenham Hotspur. But the Football Association dropped the case in August 1998 when it became clear Clough was too ill to appear before a disciplinary tribunal. Some individuals who have been investigated by the Inland Revenue are believed to have reached a private accommodation with the tax authorities.

Soccer has always attracted profiteers, for one simple reason: the amounts of cash floating around the game. In days gone by, when thousands of spectators were crammed on to open terraces and catering facilities were best described as primitive, there were plenty of opportunities for crooked club directors to siphon off large amounts of cash. One favourite ploy was to cream off a percentage of the gate receipts. If the turnstiles clicked 20,000 times, you released an official attendance figure of somewhere around 17,000 and pocketed the difference.

If a wealthy club fancied the look of an outstanding youth player being groomed by a smaller, neighbouring club, then the chief scout was instructed to offer inducements to the boy's parents to persuade him of the merits of joining the bigger club. It seldom failed. Nowadays those kinds of practices are not supposed to happen. All the major clubs have swanky, modern stadia offering gourmet food in private boxes, and computerised turnstile systems. And there are strict rules outlawing the poaching of staff from other clubs, whether they are schoolboys, experienced internationals or even managers. However, clubs repeatedly break the rules concerning illegal approaches by acting via third parties, often agents.

INTRODUCTION

Other opportunities for manipulating vast sums of money have increased thanks to ever-spiralling transfer fees, huge sponsorship agreements, multi-million pound television deals and the enormous commercial activities surrounding the game's leading clubs. Not to mention the number of clubs now flirting with the Stock Exchange. The latter explosion has allowed a small number of club owners to reap a handsome reward for what was in reality a fairly modest outlay to gain a controlling interest in the clubs' affairs. This is not to suggest that there is anything illegal about such activities. A punt on the Stock Exchange is just like any other punt, just that the sums involved are usually a lot bigger.

Gambling in sport is a huge industry, especially where soccer is concerned. As well as the popular weekly football pools, still thriving despite competition from the National Lottery, there is now a whole new variety of ways for punters to spend their money. You can stroll down to the bookmakers and lay out a modest few quid on guessing the name and the time of the first goalscorer in a particular match. If you are lucky enough to be a guest in a private box at any big game, you are almost certain to be visited before the match by an attractively dressed young lady, sporting a bookmaker's sash, offering you the same kind of service. And if you are a more ambitious punter and go in for the new craze of spread betting, you can chance your luck on such esoteric subjects as the number of corners in the first half, the number of throw-ins, the number of bookings and so on. Once you have worked out your odds and chosen your figure, any excess on that can leave you with a handsome profit. However, get your sums wrong and it can cost you a small fortune.

Footballers, and anyone connected with a club, are forbidden by FA laws from gambling on their own results.

One famous case concerning sportsmen betting against themselves featured the Australian cricket team in the 1981 'Botham Test' at Headingley. The Australians were so far ahead that one bookmaker at the ground suddenly offered odds of 500–1 against England winning the Test. Even though the Aussies were obviously going flat out to win, anything can happen in sport and these odds were simply too good to ignore in a two-horse race. During a break in play, some Australian players got their coach driver to lay a number of bets, and there followed the most spectacular batting display from Ian Botham, whose innings of a lifetime saved England from an innings defeat. The Australians were left with a fairly modest total to chase but Bob Willis produced an astonishing bowling display to roll over the tourists and leave England the most unlikely victors in Test history. The Aussies slunk away from Headingley dejected at their defeat, but with some of them several thousand pounds wealthier thanks to the freak odds offered by the bookies. Although the Australians protested that they had never let up at any stage throughout the match, once news of their betting coup leaked out they were inevitably faced with accusations that they had deliberately thrown the match.

Years later, those same charges were laid against the footballers in the dock at Winchester Crown Court. Representing Hans Segers was lawyer Mel Goldberg, a solicitor who specialized in handling the complex contractual affairs of sportsmen. He had negotiated terms for the Dutch goalkeeper during his move from Nottingham Forest to Wimbledon, the team known as the Crazy Gang, for whom Fashanu had also played.

Now Mel had a far bigger job on his hands, putting together a legal team to defend Hans Segers. If Segers was convicted, it would have meant a substantial period of imprisonment and the destruction of his life.

PART ONE

——

HANS'S STORY

1

THE DAWN RAIDS

It sounded like the house was falling down. It was 6.30am. Who on earth was banging on the door so loudly at that time of the morning?

Was it the milkman? The postman? Or maybe one of my Crazy Gang footballing colleagues from Wimbledon who had got lost on his way home from a night out?

We live in the quiet, sleepy little town of Fleet, in northern Hampshire. Whoever it was must have had a good excuse for making all that row.

My wife, Astrid, asked if I was getting up. I said: 'No, I'm still asleep. You go.'

Astrid got up and began to go downstairs to answer the door. She must have been half asleep and twisted her ankle as she slipped on the stair carpet. She cried out in pain and so I got up and threw on my dressing-gown.

She was rubbing her ankle at the top of the stairs as I yawned and passed her. I patted her on the shoulder and went towards the front door expecting to see a postman with a recorded delivery parcel or something like that to be signed for.

As I opened the door, I was greeted by the glare of bright lights and flashguns. It seemed like the whole house was surrounded by TV cameras and newspaper photographers. If this was a wind-up by my Wimbledon team-mates, it was certainly a very elaborate one.

Instead of a postman, three men and a woman were standing on the doorstep. They told me that they were from Hampshire Police. They said that I was going to be arrested for conspiracy to defraud bookmakers and that they had a search warrant.

I was in shock. Astrid called down to find out what was going on.

'What's happening?' she said. 'What's going on?'

'Don't worry,' I said. 'It's all a mistake.'

The police barged in through the front door. Once inside, the senior officer repeated that he had a warrant for my arrest. I was half asleep when I had gone to the door but his words soon woke me up. He said I was implicated in a so-called soccer match-fixing ring. I was stunned. Football has always been my life. I just couldn't believe the things they were accusing me of.

They proceeded to turn the house upside down. They looked in every room. They searched in every drawer and cupboard, and they gave particular attention to my study. They went through everything, and decided to take away several documents. These included diaries and paperwork concerning some business activities I had begun to develop in my spare-time, such as selling ties made in Holland to sports clubs in Britain. A Dutch tie-maker hoped that having a professional footballer endorsing his product and arranging introductions, would be good for business.

Footballers in Britain usually have a lot of spare time on their hands once training has finished for the day. But instead of spending that time playing snooker, or going to the races, I had intended to use my spare time more wisely and productively.

The police told Astrid and me not to speak to each other in Dutch, as we normally do, but to say anything we had to in English.

Despite all the commotion, our children, Brigitte and Nicky, remained asleep until it was time for Astrid to wake them up and take them to school. But with all the fuss, we decided it might be best to give them the day off. When they eventually woke up, we explained to them that it was nothing to worry about and that Daddy was just helping the police.

I went upstairs to get dressed and more embarrassment followed, with a policeman waiting at my bedroom door. I couldn't believe all this was happening. It looked just like a scene from a film. My head was spinning. All sorts of thoughts were colliding with each other as I tried to come to terms with what was happening. I was still wondering who had tipped off the press to be outside my front door at that time of the morning.

The policewoman then went upstairs with my wife and searched through my belongings. Astrid was allowed to get dressed, again with the policewoman waiting by the door. This intrusion was unbelievable. The experience of having people doing this, inside my house, made me feel sick and angry.

At around 9.30am I was taken from my home to Eastleigh police station, near Southampton. I was told I was to answer charges of being involved in a plot to rig the results of games in the English Premier League.

When I left the house, I told Astrid not to worry and that I expected I would soon be home. What I didn't know was that a number of other police operations had been arranged to coincide that morning. Also arrested were my Wimbledon team-mate John Fashanu, his girlfriend Melissa (later to become his wife), Bruce Grobbelaar, the Southampton and former Liverpool goalkeeper, and a Malaysian businessman called Richard Lim.

The arrests followed a newspaper 'sting' operation several months earlier that was set up by *The Sun* and Grobbelaar's former business partner Chris Vincent. Bruce had apparently sunk a lot of money into a game reserve venture in Zimbabwe that was being promoted by Vincent, who was always on the lookout for new investors in Britain. But when the business failed to get off the ground, and Bruce's donations dried up, the two men fell out and

Vincent turned against his former friend in a vicious and spiteful manner. Broke and desperate, having apparently squandered all the money Bruce had invested, Vincent contacted *The Sun* and offered them a story about Grobbelaar supposedly receiving huge sums of cash from a Far Eastern gambling syndicate in return for attempting to fix the results of matches.

The Sun decided to run with the story but they needed 'evidence' to back up Vincent's claims. So they went to elaborate lengths to bug a hotel room to obtain videotape evidence of conversations between Grobbelaar and Vincent. Once they had published a series of stories detailing their allegations in graphic tabloid fashion, they then handed over their dossier of 'evidence' to the police and the whole operation escalated into a whirlwind that engulfed so many people and threatened to destroy their lives – and the lives of those close to them.

It was the beginning of the worst time of my life. Two and a half years of hell as I fought to prove my innocence. It was a living nightmare that threatened to ruin my career, my marriage, and put me behind bars.

2

EARLY YEARS IN
HOLLAND

I was born Hans Johannes Cornelius Antonius Segers on 30
October 1961 in the Dutch city of Eindhoven. Eindhoven is a
bustling city in the southern Netherlands, not far from the Belgian
border. It is a big industrial centre, with most employment being
in the electrical, motor vehicle, tobacco and textiles sectors.

My father, Theo Segers, was born in 1939. He worked all his life
for Philips, the multinational electrical company based in Eindhoven. They have a controlling interest in the local football team
– so now you know what the P stands for in PSV Eindhoven. Ask
the majority of people in Eindhoven where they work and they
will all tell you the same thing: Philips. The PSV stadium is right
next door to the big Philips factory. It always was a fantastic
stadium and is now one of the most modern in Europe, with
new stands all the way round. Needless to say, the floodlights are
provided by Philips as well. In fact, Philips now produce some of
the most advanced floodlighting systems in the business and they
are installed at many of the world's major stadiums.

Dad was an electrical engineer who often worked abroad, including many times in China. He was a very keen footballer in his younger days and played in the reserves for Eindhoven, the second club in the city after PSV. Now they are in the First Division, while PSV battle for supremacy in the Premier with the likes of Ajax and Feyenoord. Dad was a full-back. He was a small man, but, to use a familiar Dutch expression, he was made of concrete. He played on well into his forties, but two broken legs in the space of a year ended his footballing days. He is a very hard worker in his job, and I remember that he always worked long hours to look after the children and pay the bills. I have a huge amount of respect for the way he has conducted his life, and the way he has looked after my mother and my family.

My mother, Tonnie, was a war baby, born in 1943. She had me when she was eighteen years old. Like my dad, she has always been a hard-working person, bringing up three children and, incredibly, she is still working to this day. She says that the four hours a day she puts in always pays for the holidays she enjoys with Dad. I love her to bits. She has always been there for us and the one regret I have about living in England is that I miss having my family around.

I was the oldest of the three children and next in line is my brother Frank, born in 1965. Like me, he was a promising footballer in his younger days. But it was easy to see that he lacked the skills required to play at the very highest level. He was incredibly fit and switched his sporting attentions to athletics and became a gifted runner, concentrating on the 200 metres and 400 metres. Frank is now working as a driver. He is married with two children, a lovely family. He has a heart of gold and nothing seems to be too much trouble for him. My father always used to say that he wished Frank had had my competitiveness, that will to win which seemed to come naturally to me. That's what I had. I always wanted to win.

I hated to lose, even at board games. We had a game similar to snakes and ladders, with sixty squares on it. Number 21 had a picture of a well and if you landed on it you had to miss three goes. Whenever I landed on that square I started crying. I loved playing the game but I remember getting a pair of scissors and cutting out square number 21. And even when I was small and playing in goal, I remember I would cry when I let a goal in.

My other brother is Marco, born in 1972. I have always had a special relationship with him, probably because he is the youngest. I always used to look after him while my parents were out. I remember the day he was born. He was such a sweet kid.

Marco also took up football and he definitely had a bit more skill than Frank. He had the potential to be a brilliant player but, like Frank, he just did not have that desire to win that is a crucial part of the make-up of any top sportsman. He is still keen on football, though, and often comes over to England to stay with us and to watch me play. That love of sport certainly runs in our family. One of my nephews on my mother's side also played professionally with Eindhoven.

Whenever my family get together and talk about the old days, my mother still reminds me about my earliest times at school. I must admit that I hated school. Even in my nursery school days, I would often simply refuse to go. There were several shops between home and the school and if we stopped off at one on the way, my mother couldn't get me out. I would cling on to anything to delay the inevitable.

I think that particular spell coloured my thoughts of school for the next ten years or so. Nowadays I am sure I would be diagnosed as clinically hyperactive and maybe put on medication to help me to concentrate in class. When I was nine or ten, my mother took me to see an educational psychologist, who sat me down and got me playing games to see how long I could concentrate on one particular task. I don't think she knew what to suggest to help. Certainly there were no special exclusion diets or tablets in those days to help hyperactive children.

To call me an underachiever at school would be putting it politely. I must admit I found it hard to sit still in class and listen to lessons for hours on end and then go home and do my homework. Every year was a real struggle, but somehow I got through it all. I suppose I was a bit of a Jack the Lad at school, throwing my weight around and not worrying too much about passing any exams. It wasn't good for my education – but ideal training for my later career in England with Wimbledon's Crazy Gang.

Luckily, I was good at English and we had a great teacher called Mr Wim van Wijk. He was quite a young guy and fitted in just like one of the boys. I am sure he would have liked it at Wimbledon, too! PE was definitely my favourite subject for the simple reason that I loved all sports. But I was always in trouble with my German teacher, Mr Hoppenbrouwer. Nothing used to stop me talking usually, but I was terrified to say anything in his classes. I found it impossible to sit still and I was always in trouble for fidgeting or looking out of the window. I hated German so much that I was always skipping lessons. When it came to German exams, I would often sneak in a book and copy out the answers. Needless to say, I was a regular visitor to the headmaster's office for getting into trouble in classes and detention would usually follow as a punishment.

The best thing about school was easy to define: that's where I met my wife, Astrid. We still laugh about one particular incident when she was being chased by a boy who started throwing snowballs at her. When he came along the corridor back into school, I simply picked him up, stuck a coathanger inside his jacket – while he was still wearing it – and hung him up on the wall. I will never forget the sight of him hanging there with his arms and legs waving in the air . . .

Despite living in Eindhoven, I was really an Ajax supporter. I went to watch them between the ages of 13 and 15. I used to go with a friend from the neighbourhood, Barend, who was six or seven years older than me. He was an absolute Ajax fanatic. He used to take me on the train to home matches in Amsterdam and without doubt my favourite Ajax player was the incredible Johan Cruyff. Another sporting hero of mine was the world heavyweight boxing champion Muhammad Ali. I remember watching some of his fights when it was way past my bedtime. Sometimes I would creep out of bed in the middle of the night and tiptoe downstairs to turn on the TV to watch his fights. A real legend, and an incredible man.

Only one thing helped me to get through my homework. The quicker I did it, the sooner I could go outside and join my friends playing football.

I started playing football when I was about ten years old and joined a neighbourhood amateur club called Woensel. One of my favourite players when I was a child was a man called Jan van Beveren, the PSV Eindhoven goalkeeper. He was a great athlete and performed like a cat, flying through the air to make magnificent saves. Van Beveren was a real joy to watch and I guess he must have given me the inspiration to become a goalkeeper myself. It was a real thrill to meet him when I joined PSV at the age of sixteen. Even better than that was to be invited to train with my hero on a few occasions when I was called up to practise with the first team squad. That really was a dream come true.

Woensel had the highest membership of any junior club in the country and were quite influential in youth football in the region. I remember from the early days there were two coaches who came on motorbikes to training and matches. I played three or four matches in goal for the under-11 team and must have impressed them because pretty soon I was moved up to the next age group.

Our Woensel team won a lot of league championships and knockout tournaments, which was a terrific achievement considering professional clubs like Ajax and PSV also had teams in the same competitions. The Dutch youth football system is very different from England's. You can join a professional club from a very young age. To beat the junior teams from one of the big clubs was a great feeling.

At the age of thirteen or fourteen, I was already involved in a great rivalry with another goalkeeper, Peter van Rooij. He was a year older than me and played in the division above. On Tuesdays and Thursdays we would have specialist goalkeeper training together from Jan van Gennip, who was one of the dads. Jan never played in goal himself but he thought I was a good prospect. Most of the time in training seemed to be taken up with stopping shots.

For a while I played as a full-back, like my father, of course. I wanted to try and emulate him but we didn't win those matches so I soon went back in goal. I remember we won the next game and the manager was pleased with my performance. After that, I stayed between the posts for the club team.

I was also in the school team but we had three good goalkeepers, all in the same class. After discussions with my teacher, who was also a coach, we decided that I would play outfield, as a sweeper. I was captain of my school team and I really enjoyed playing in that position. The experience of playing sweeper in those early days was another thing that came in handy later on when I played for Wimbledon, tidying up behind the defence and getting the ball back down to the other end of the field as soon as possible. Our school team did very well in junior tournaments, frequently winning competitions against teams who were a year older than us.

When I was sixteen, I heard that PSV had been watching me for quite a few weeks. The man who was scouting on me was their specialist goalkeeping coach, Willy Heyink. Just before that, my big rival Peter van Rooij was invited to go for a trial with Feyenoord of Rotterdam. Amazingly, he decided not to go and concentrate on his schoolwork instead. Feeling about school the way I did, I just couldn't believe it. My chance came a little later.

I was absolutely thrilled to join my hometown professional club. I was under coach Jan Reker, who later became the main coach of PSV. Willy, the goalkeeping coach, was nicknamed *Het Kanon*, which is Dutch for 'The Cannon' – and believe me, his shots felt as if they had been fired at you from a cannon. From doing schoolwork every day to training every day was a wonderful change of lifestyle, and my passion for football took over my whole life.

While I was still at school, my lessons came second to football. I had only one thing on my mind, to become a professional foot-baller. My dad wasn't happy about it and tried to persuade me that school should still come first, just in case anything went wrong at PSV. Don't put all your eggs in one basket, he said. But I took no notice. Football was my life, I lived for football. No drinking. No nightclubs. Just my football, and my girlfriend, Astrid . . .

I remember seeing Astrid when I was 16 but it was another year before I spoke to her properly. Astrid was then 13. She lived across the road, so we were about 300 metres apart from each other. At school I was always trying to impress her, but it didn't work at first. Her parents were worried because Astrid was three years younger than me. We were forbidden to see each other for a while, so I would use any excuse I could to get close to her. After school, my friends and I used to play football in a field outside Astrid's house and we used two trees as the goalposts. If the ball ever went towards Astrid's house, it was always me who ran in that direction to fetch it! Naturally, I would always look towards the windows as I did so and Astrid's mother soon noticed my antics.

When I was chosen to play for PSV, it became the talk of the school. That *did* impress Astrid. I was very persistent as a suitor and Astrid and I became very fond of each other. Astrid tells me she thought I was quite cute. Her father began to take her to watch me play for the PSV youth and reserve teams. Between the ages of sixteen and eighteen I was training with PSV every day after school, usually between 5pm and 7pm. The training ground was outside the town and it used to take me about twenty-five minutes to get there on my pushbike.

In the early days my mum used to wash my kit, and she hated it. In the winter I would come home covered in mud from top to toe. She would make me rinse my kit in a bucket in the garage to get the mud out before putting any of it into the washing machine. (Being connected with Philips you get to know a thing or two about washing machines. They normally last about eight years but, because of all my muddy kit, ours packed up after three. I guess I still owe Mum a new washing machine.) We had to buy our own boots but the rest of the kit was provided by the club. It was such a professional set-up and everything was arranged for you.

My first contract with PSV was in 1979, when I left school at eighteen. Signing with one of the biggest clubs in Holland and

Europe was a dream come true. That first contract was worth £100 a week. My dad came along with me when I signed. He had no experience in negotiating contracts, but who cared? I was a professional footballer with PSV. Looking back, I realize how much my own father criticized me. But on reflection, that was quite a positive thing. He didn't want to spoil me, just to protect me. He was always a perfectionist. That's the way Dad is with everything, with work and all aspects of his life.

When I finished school, as well as training with the club I began working in the Philips staff shop, where members of the Philips workforce could buy products at reduced prices. I worked in the shop during the mornings and trained in the afternoons.

Nearly everyone in Holland has a bike. But by this time I had got round to borrowing my dad's moped. (He never got round to passing his full driving test – and still hasn't.) After training, the PSV boys often went into town to hang out around the red light area, having fun as kids do, drinking Coke and chatting to the girls.

I was joined at PSV by another former Woensel player, Frans van Rooij, the brother of Peter. That was nice. We were team-mates at Woensel for four or five years and it was good for the club to have two players graduate through to the professional ranks.

After sharing my football with a job in the shop, at the age of twenty my football had to fit in with National Service. It lasted fourteen months and was then compulsory in Holland, but it has since been abolished.

Army training started at Venlo in the south of the country, about forty-five minutes from Eindhoven. I trained with a local team, VVV Venlo, three times a week, and returned home at weekends to play for PSV reserves. After basic training we moved to a perma- nent camp at Oirschot, which was just five minutes away from the PSV training ground. I was given a job as chauffeur to the captain of our regiment. I had passed my driving test at the age of eighteen and here I was, whizzing around in Army Land Rovers. Fortunately the captain was a very keen sportsman, a marathon runner, and we got on together very well. He really looked after me and often gave me time off if I had a midweek reserve match.

After several years in the reserves, waiting patiently for my big chance, I finally got the call-up to the first team when I was twenty-two. That's young for a goalkeeper. I remember playing for the reserves on the Saturday afternoon and getting a call to join the first team later that evening to meet up with the rest of the players before the match on the Sunday. I was called up because Pim Doesburg, the Dutch international goalkeeper, was not enjoying the best of form. I made my debut as a second-half substitute against MVV Maastricht. The Maastricht stadium was a real dump, not unlike Wimbledon's old ground. But it was still a special day for me, a young boy from Eindhoven playing for such a big club.

It was an end-of-season match and we won 7–1. The weather was miserable and I remember the wind and rain more than anything special about the match, only that we were comfortably ahead and the coach was just giving me a run-out to see how I performed. Two other players made their debuts that day: Barry van Aarle, a defender, and Edwin van den Bergenhenegouwen, a midfielder with one of the longest names in football. It was a good job he never got a transfer to England. There would not have been enough room on his shirt to get the name on the back!

After playing at MVV I was back in the reserve team, but it was nice to get a taste of first team football and thrilling to play alongside so many fantastic footballers. Normally, I am not a nervous person, but I certainly was in those early days in the first team. Frank and I were the only players from Eindhoven in the team and I think that puts you in the spotlight even more. The positive things were that all our family and friends came to watch all the matches and the support we received was tremendous. We had a team full of internationals, including Doesburg, the twin brothers Rene and Willy van der Kerkhof, Ruud Geels, Pietr Wiltschut, Ernie Brandts, Jan Poortvliet, Huub Stevens, Arie Haan, Danish international Jan Heintze and the Norwegian captain Halvar Thoresen. Rene was a tremendous player, and famous for playing in the World Cup final in Argentina in 1978 with a broken hand. His brother Willy is now a successful businessman.

Two or three of them really went out of their way to help me settle in. Stevens, who became manager at German club Schalke 04, Brandts, who remained at PSV as a coach, and Willy all gave me a lot of advice in training. It really opened your eyes working with guys who had so much experience. They were so dedicated. They trained the way they played, with total commitment. They were a great example to follow. Of all the advice I was given, I remember Willy saying that in football you can win an important championship today and tomorrow you could be out on the street.

It summed up the precarious nature of this job. And it emphasized the fact that you can never afford to let your standards slip, either while playing or in training. It is such a short career and you need luck, especially with contracts and transfers, and most of all by staying clear of injuries.

I made my full debut in January 1982 in a local derby at home to Helmond Sport. We won 3–1 and again I remember the conditions were horrendous. It was freezing cold, there was a blizzard and you could hardly see through the driving snow. I know I didn't play particularly well, but I stayed in the team for the remainder of the season.

The highlight of my time with PSV was the match away to Ajax. For me, having supported them as a boy, it was a very special occasion. In England, before big games, clubs often take their players away to a hotel the night before a match. But as Holland is such a small country, we drove everywhere on the day of the match. PSV did everything in style. They had a luxury coach and it was wonderful driving through the crowds to the Ajax stadium in Amsterdam. Ajax had a star-studded team including Marco van Basten, Frank Rijkaard and the long-serving Stanley Menzo in goal. It was a desperately close game and the only goal was scored by van Basten. I closed him down as he came into the area but he still managed to find the far corner with a stunning shot. At that time he was one of the best finishers in the world. He moved on to play for AC Milan in Italy but never recovered from an ankle injury.

Another magical memory was the 1-1 home draw against Feyenoord. Johan Cruyff played for them that season and although he was nearing the end of his career, he was still the best player on the park. With such incredible skill, vision and technique, he ran the show. Cruyff helped Feyenoord to the title that year, with Ajax finishing second and PSV third. Another great day I remember was my first European match, against Ferencvaros from Hungary. We were drawn away in the UEFA Cup and won 2-0. It was wonderful being part of a team with so many outstanding and talented players, and you knew you had to perform at the highest level to be accepted as part of the team. That was real pressure. Frans van Rooij was a good friend of mine, especially as we grew up together through the Woensel team before joining PSV. Other good friends were Marc Pauly and Edwin van der Bergen Henegouwen. Both players came from the PSV youth teams. We always travelled together and after matches went out together in a group.

It's funny, but all through my life I have known what I have wanted to achieve and gone out to get it. I always wanted to be a professional footballer, and made that wish come true. And even as a sixteen-year-old, I knew that one day Astrid was going to be my wife.

They say that love will find a way. Well, even when we were not allowed to see each other we became quite skilled at managing to arrange secret dates. And I became skilled at climbing in and out of windows and up drainpipes into Astrid's room. However, I was frequently caught out by her mother, Annie, who often saw my footprints on the veranda. At other times we used to meet in a playground and hide in the bushes while Astrid's mother rode round and round on her bike looking for us. She knew what was going on and was really good about it. Underneath everything, all she was trying to do was to love and protect her daughter. Astrid was the youngest of seven children and her mother was forty-two and her father fifty-six when she was born. What you might call an accident, which might account for why her mother was so protective towards her. Sadly, Astrid's father had had a stroke and was left with slight problems with his speech. Tragically, he died of a blood clot on the brain while Astrid was still at school.

Astrid and I did split up for about two years and I had two other girlfriends during that time, but I always kept in touch with Astrid and still saw her on a regular basis. When she and I got back together again, we started going out to nightclubs and discos on Saturdays after the football. I have never been a big beer-drinker. Just an occasional lager is fine for me. I never had more than two or three drinks. If I had done, I think I would have had problems finding the car afterwards . . .

When I was twenty I was growing a little rebellious at home and there were often flashpoints because of my behaviour being in total contrast to my father's strictness. If he had said dinner was to be on the table at 5pm then it was, but sometimes I would not roll in until seven, eight or nine o'clock. There were frequent bust-ups between my father and myself and so I was looking to move out. Astrid and I talked things over with her mother and the upshot was that I moved out of the family home and moved in with Astrid and her mother. All of her other children had grown up and left home, and Annie now has more than twenty grandchildren. It was wonderful to be together with Astrid, and I suppose it was good for Annie to have a man about the house again. I used to help wash up and cut the grass, but I never got involved in any cooking. My culinary skills have rarely extended beyond making toast or opening packets of biscuits.

Less than a year after moving in with Astrid, I was on the move again. To Nottingham.

3

LIFE UNDER CLOUGHIE

My world collapsed on 5 December 1983. In Holland, that day is a celebration of St Nicholas, when children receive presents. My present that day was the news that PSV had agreed to sign Hans van Breukelen from Nottingham Forest to be the number one goalkeeper the following season.

After several months in the first team, I had hoped to be the regular goalkeeper myself, and as a local lad who had worked his way up through the PSV system, I just couldn't face a future of sitting on the bench as a substitute or playing in the reserves. That kind of existence does you no good as a player. You lose the sharpness and competitiveness you get from regular first-team football.

With Pim Doesburg reaching the twilight of his playing days, I had hoped that the goalkeeper's position would be mine for the rest of my career. But looking back, I have to admit that I was not playing well enough for a club of the calibre of PSV. During the summer the club had received a number of offers for me from small Division Two clubs in Holland, with crowds of around three or four thousand. But I didn't fancy that one little bit. After working so hard to get where I was, I was not prepared to start playing at a lower level.

I trained with van Breukelen in pre-season and before I met him, I thought: 'You bastard, you have taken my job.' But after meeting him I soon found out that Hans was the nicest kind of guy you could meet, very friendly and understanding, blessed with a great personality and superb goalkeeping skills. That particular episode taught me another lesson in life. Never judge people.

One day Hans came up to me and said that Nottingham Forest were still looking for a replacement goalkeeper and asked if would I be interested in a move there. He said he would phone Brian Clough, the Forest manager, on my behalf.

When he called, Hans actually got through to Alan Hill, the assistant manager. Hill called and told me that Hans had recommended me, and offered me the opportunity to go to Forest for a four-week trial. I was so excited. This was another dream, to play for one of the biggest clubs in England, a team who had won the European Cup. As a kid I had watched a lot of English clubs on television and had become a big admirer of Ray Clemence, of Liverpool, Tottenham and England.

I flew to East Midlands airport, where Alan Hill was waiting for me. My English career had begun. Forest were in pre-season training at the time and there was another goalkeeper, from Belgium, there on trial. After five days of training, and playing in one friendly match, I was told by Forest that they wanted me to sign a contract. My agent, Gerry Lagendijk, came over and told me Forest wanted to sign me on loan from PSV for one year. I thought, OK, one year in England is no problem. I was really looking forward to it, this new opening in a foreign country where the standard of football is so high and there are so many big and famous clubs. If you are going to prove yourself anywhere, then this is the place to do it.

I discussed the move with Astrid and she was happy to come over with me to England for a year. But after a while, I remember saying I had a feeling inside me that this move was more likely to be for ten years than one year. No way, she said. Put it down to my impulsive nature, if you like, but by now I had learned to trust my instinct.

The goalkeeper at Forest was Steve Sutton, a former understudy to the great Peter Shilton and van Breukelen. After a few months, I was getting restless because I wasn't playing in the first team. I had come to England to play. That was why I had left the comfort and security of life in Eindhoven. But in November 1984 came a breakthrough. After a spell of nine games when Forest went without a win, Brian Clough put me in against Coventry away and I played a blinder as we broke our barren spell with a vital 3-1 win. I could not have asked for a better start, and still count that match as one of my favourites.

Forest had a pretty solid defence and it was a pleasure playing behind guys like Paul Hart, Gary Mills and Kenny Swain. Ian Bowyer, the captain, was a real hard man, a great workhorse and often a good finisher. Steve Hodge was a fantastic, skilful player, and Garry Birtles had a great spell as a striker at Forest before being sold to Manchester United, where things did not turn out quite so well for him and he returned to the club.

In March the next year, 1985, Astrid and I decided to get married. My best present that time was a permanent contract with Forest for three years. So one year in England soon became four. My instinct was heading in the right direction.

Most of the contract negotiations were dealt with by my agent, who also represented van Breukelen. During one of the transfer meetings, I remember the manager of PSV Eindhoven sitting in Brian Clough's office. Cloughie came up to me and said, 'Who's that man in my office?' Clough had a fierce temper and a very abrasive attitude towards most people and most situations. He didn't care who he upset. This Dutchman was 6ft 6in tall, but by the time Cloughie had finished shouting at him for sitting in his chair, he must have felt about five feet tall!

One day, when we were away to West Ham United, we got stuck in a huge traffic jam on the notorious M25 motorway, to the north of London. There were heavy roadworks, with cones everywhere but not a roadworker in sight as it was a Saturday. Cloughie jumped down off the coach and moved two cones out of the way so that we could squeeze through on to a lane that wasn't being used. He told our driver, Albert, to drive along this empty lane, but Albert wasn't at all sure about this scheme. He was afraid he might lose his licence. Anyway, under orders from Cloughie he swung over into the next lane and carried on driving after the boss had put the cones back where they belonged.

As we began to make some progress, past a long line of stationary vehicles, we saw a police car heading straight towards us with blue lights flashing. Albert was understandably nervous but Cloughie said, 'Leave this to me.' He stepped down off the coach to speak to the two police officers and persuaded them to turn their car round and give us a police escort all the way round the M25! We arrived at the ground with about twenty minutes to spare before the kick-off.

One of life's coincidences meant that John Fashanu's brother, Justin, was also at Nottingham Forest, after Cloughie had splashed out £1million to sign him from Norwich City. One day, Justin decided that he wanted to put in some extra time on the training pitch, but Cloughie refused him permission. Justin went along anyway, but after kicking a few balls around he was ordered off the pitch. Cloughie had phoned the police and asked them to escort Justin from the training ground. I am sure everyone in soccer was stunned by the news of Justin's recent tragic death.

Justin may have cost £1million, but to Cloughie there were no such things as star players. He was the main man and ruled with fear. I was fortunate that he seemed to like me. In fact, he seemed to like Dutch players in general, maybe because we were used to hard work. Anyway, at times I saw him turn against players he took a dislike to and absolutely slaughter them verbally. One player, Gary Megson, was bought and sold six months later without playing a single game – just because Cloughie turned against him almost immediately after signing him.

Life under Cloughie was often amazing. He was a legend in

Nottingham and was as popular as Robin Hood! You always felt his presence in and around the club. For someone who had amassed considerable wealth from his success in the game, it was amazing to see the way he dressed. On match days, during meetings and outside football, his green top and blue tracksuit bottoms were his trademark. Most managers are seen with a suit and tie most of the time, but not Cloughie. Everybody was afraid of him, except for one, Johnny Metgod, an experienced Dutch player, and a man with his own views of life, inside and outside of football. John and his wife Patty were a great help to Astrid and me during my time with Forest and we developed a real friendship. Their advice certainly helped us to cope with the move to Nottingham.

Clough was a great motivator. He would often go away fishing for a week and then turn up in the dressing-room at ten to three before an important match and just walk round to individual players telling them how he wanted them to perform. Nearly always, his talks ended with the words: Keep it simple. He always said it, over and over again. Just do the thing you get paid for. If you are a right-back, then play as a right-back. If you are a goal-keeper, you are paid to catch the ball. If you are a centre-half, you are paid to defend and head the ball. If you play in midfield and you are a good tackler, your job is to win the ball and give it to a team-mate who is good at passing. If you are a striker, you should keep it simple and let the ball do the work. Those were his commandments. Very simple but true – and very effective.

However, when it came to tactical analysis, planning free-kicks and corners or defending certain areas, he was not so good. He didn't use to worry about finding out about other teams. Or at least if he did, he certainly didn't let on. This kind of information was just never discussed. This was the most amazing thing about coming to England. At PSV I was part of one of the top teams in Holland, who were well-organized and thoroughly professional in every department. Once I had become a senior player at PSV, my mother was delighted when I stopped bringing kit home to be washed and the club took care of it every day. There was not the same luxury at Forest. Instead of washing the kit every day after training, they would usually hang it up in the drying room. The smell in that place was unbearable and some of my kit was as stiff as a board when I had to put it on again, unwashed, the next day.

It took some time to get used to the different way of life at a leading English club and it was a very frustrating time at first. The training facilities were poor and so was the standard of training. We would often spend most of our time playing the sort of games you might expect to see in a school playground, lining up in teams, passing the ball through your legs to somebody behind, who would pass the ball over his head to the next player, who would pass it through his legs, and so on. We would do that for a while and then finish up with a small five-a-side game. There was hardly any specialist goalkeeping work, so I would usually play outfield in the five-a-sides. By the time I left Forest I was probably one of the best finishers in the club! At one stage Cloughie thought of making me a permanent substitute (we only had one player on the bench in those days) so I could come on as a goalkeeper or as an outfield player.

At the time of writing, it is very sad to see Cloughie in such poor health and I was glad to see the FA drop the charges against him of accepting transfer bungs. I couldn't see what the FA were trying to achieve in pressing charges against him. He has retired from the game now and has nothing to do with football any more. I suspect they were setting him up to try and make an example of him. That's the way I felt the authorities behaved towards us in the trial, so I sympathize with his predicament.

Clough's way with players was really just kidology, nothing more. Behind that angry façade, he is a real gentleman. He should be allowed to enjoy his retirement and be left in peace. All sorts of allegations have been made about the way he conducted his transfers. Well, all I can say is that I never saw any brown envelopes change hands or any evidence of this kind of activity in my time at Forest, although it is common knowledge that this sort of thing does go on throughout Europe. In short, managers ought to be able to reap the benefits of their transfer activities in terms of bonuses. It's good business for the club, and if a manager's skills in the transfer market make the club better off, then it is only fair for him to receive a performance-related bonus.

When it comes to transfers and contracts, players like to keep things private, and that's the way it should be. In all my years as a professional footballer, I think I have only known what one or two other players have earned. It's their business, not mine, and vice-versa.

When we first moved to England we lived in a small village called Cotgrave, near Nottingham. We enjoyed life there. Astrid and I were together on our own for the first time, and in a strange country. At first we found it hard to settle down, but things certainly improved after I had made a successful debut in the first team. After all, as I said before, I had not come to England to sit around in the reserves. Astrid was feeling lonely and so we got ourselves a puppy, a beautiful black labrador which we named Lucky. Astrid always wanted a dog and Rocky helped her to make life more enjoyable.

England overall was what we expected. We had to get used to the non-stop rain as well as the strange language and especially the accent, but we found the people very friendly and helpful. Alan Hill was a really nice man. He and the coaches, Ronnie Fenton and Liam O'Kane, helped us with advice about buying a house, which was a big investment for us to make. We felt the English people were very friendly, polite and helpful, but rather reserved. They keep things to themselves. We found it strange when we wanted to visit people and had to telephone to make an appointment. In Holland you just come around when you feel like it.

Once I was established in the first team, the football was everything I had imagined it would be: absolutely brilliant. The passion, the atmosphere and the huge crowds. Another dream come true, to be part of such an exciting set-up.

We made some good friends in our first home in Cotgrave, and I soon got used to the amount of free time enjoyed by professional footballers in England. Instead of training twice or three times a day, as we did in Holland, we would be finished after a couple of hours and the afternoons were always free. One of our neighbours was a keen snooker player and he and I would often play in the afternoons.

I felt we had settled in reasonably well, but Astrid wasn't happy. She was homesick. She missed her family and so we reached the decision to start one of our own. Brigitte was born in Nottingham on 25 July 1985. We had just moved from Cotgrave and bought our first house together in Woollaton Park, Nottingham. We had only moved in a few weeks before Brigitte was born, five or six weeks early.

I couldn't believe how old-fashioned the conditions were at the hospital. Waiting in the emergency area, I was sitting next to one guy with a broken leg and on the other side was somebody else dripping with blood. When it came down to hygiene, it seemed that facilities in England were at least ten years behind what I was used to in Europe, so it was a worrying time for us with Astrid being in that particular hospital. There is such a huge difference between the two countries. BUPA hospitals in Britain are just like the NHS hospitals are in Holland, where you are so well looked after and you can choose whatever you want to eat. The hospital food in Nottingham was not to be recommended. To make matters worse, Astrid endured a difficult time with the birth. She was suffering from high blood pressure and when it came to the actual delivery, it took a long time to get the contractions going and the baby had to be induced.

When I saw Brigitte, I cried and cried. It was such an unbelievable experience to see your own child for the first time. Your own flesh and blood, a real, living miracle. It was the best day of my life, with vivid memories I know I will never, ever forget. Despite the conditions, the nursing staff were absolutely brilliant.

Being a proud father was an incredibly enlightening, spiritual experience. But I still had a job to do, part of which meant getting a good night's sleep before matches. So, to avoid being kept awake by the baby's crying, I used to sleep in the spare bedroom on Friday nights.

Brigitte developed a stomach valve problem in her first few

months and found it difficult to keep her food down. It was a very nerve-racking period in our lives and at one time Brigitte turned yellow and had to go back into hospital into an incubator. A specialist prescribed some powder which helped the food solidify when it reached her stomach so that she wouldn't bring it all back up again. Luckily, in time, the condition healed up on its own.

Nicky was born nearly three years later, on 14 April 1988. He was also born in Nottingham, but at a different hospital. Nicky's birth was a more frightening experience. Astrid was almost eight months into her pregnancy when all of a sudden she started bleeding. The doctor decided that Astrid's condition was too dangerous for the baby and directed a Caesarean delivery. I was present in the delivery room while the Caesarean was done and I witnessed the whole operation. I couldn't believe how many layers they have to cut through, just like a butcher cutting through meat. Then, all of a sudden, they grabbed his feet and pulled him out and we both shouted, 'Oh, it's a boy.'

We had wanted a boy and were both overjoyed. Despite being born five weeks prematurely, Nicky was a healthy 5lb 4oz, a couple of ounces heavier than Brigitte was when she was born. Nicky was another unhappy baby who cried all though the night. He also had a stomach problem and seemed to be in a lot of pain all the time. Once again we were going back and forth to doctors and specialists. And once again I was sleeping in the spare room on Friday nights.

Each birth was a very special, emotional time. And each time, Astrid's mother, Annie, came over to help out. Luckily, Astrid's blood pressure went straight back down after each birth. She has always been keen on exercise classes and aerobics, and she managed to get her figure back fairly quickly. I must admit that changing nappies was not one of my strong points. Luckily, Annie was there to help out.

As the children have grown, each one has developed a love for sport. Brigitte is very competitive and I see a lot of myself in her, especially when we play cards and she storms away from the table if she loses! When that happens, I can begin to understand how annoying my behaviour must have been for my own parents. Nicky is very keen to be a footballer and if he is able to follow in my footsteps, that would be great. Footballers enjoy a marvellous lifestyle and to be paid for your hobby is a wonderful thing. But at the end of the day, it is up to him.

4

JOINING THE CRAZY GANG

A goalkeeper's life is a precarious one. All clubs need to have at least two top-class keepers on their staff to cover for injuries or loss of form. At Nottingham, I was a regular fixture in the side throughout the 1984-5 season, but the following year, after an injury, I lost my place in the team to Steve Sutton.

I wanted to play but I wasn't being picked, so I knocked on Brian Clough's door and explained how I felt. He understood and let me go to Stoke City on loan for one match when their goal-keeper, Peter Fox, was injured. I then went on loan to Sheffield United for three months. I enjoyed it there and felt I played well, certainly well enough for them to think about signing me on a permanent basis. Had they been able to come up with the money, I am sure I would have moved to Bramall Lane. At the end of the season, I enjoyed my first taste of Scottish football when I went on loan to Dunfermline. I would go up on the Friday before the game and fly home on the Sunday morning.

When we resumed pre-season training I was on a week-to-week

contract with Forest and was looking for another club. I went to Belgium for a week with RC Genk but they had too many foreign players on their books already and the deal fell through. After playing three reserve team games at the start of the season, I got a call from Nottingham Forest to say that Wimbledon were interested in signing me. I wanted to move there straight away. But, after four years in Nottingham, Astrid felt she had had enough of England. She still wanted to go home, and we talked long and hard about my career and where it would be best to go next. Eventually, she agreed that we could make a new life in London. The big city.

I met Bobby Gould, then the Wimbledon manager, on the same day as I received the telephone call from the club. That was in September 1988. We discussed terms and, after more discussions with Astrid, I agreed to join them a week later.

Moving to Wimbledon was an immediate success story for me – on the field. The club had played five games at the start of the season with four defeats and one draw. I made my debut for them against Everton and we won 2-1. I remember taking our first free-kick, just outside our own penalty area, and I hit the ball long and hard upfield. Big John Fashanu got on the end of it and headed the ball in. It was a perfect start for me and the I think the crowd accepted me straight away. Little did Fash and I realize that years later we would be sitting side by side in the dock. Life is full of these amazing coincidences. The man who organized my defence in that trial was also the man who negotiated my transfer from Nottingham to Wimbledon, Mel Goldberg. I was introduced to him through my agent, Josephine Kirran. She worked with Mel Stein, Paul Gascoigne's agent. Jo looked after my off-field activities and Mel looked after the legal side, making sure all my contracts were both beneficial and watertight.

I settled in well with the team at Wimbledon, but off the field it was a nightmare. I spent the first two weeks in a hotel while Astrid and the children went back to Holland until I found a new house for us. That wasn't easy, in a city as big as London, and with property prices considerably higher than they were in the East

Midlands. After two weeks I moved into digs with a team-mate, Robbie Turner. It was a filthy place and the rooms were cold. I stayed there for two months while I searched for a house.

I was house-hunting virtually every day of the week until I struck lucky. I found a lovely, modern house in Fleet, near the M3 on the Hampshire-Surrey border, where we have been delighted to bring up our two children.

Joining Wimbledon, I soon saw that the two main men at the club were Vinnie Jones and John Fashanu, especially Fash. He was the captain and had a great presence, a real aura, as well as tremendous physique. As for Vinnie, my initial impression was simple: I thought he was a nutcase. But his attitude towards the game was great for team spirit, and he really was one of the lads. Fash, in contrast, was a real businessman and a natural leader. I ended up liking them both enormously.

Before you join a club, you hear all sorts of rumours about them, especially a club like Wimbledon, who had risen from non-league football to win the FA Cup in a very short space of time, scrapping their way up through the divisions and not caring about the reputations of the big clubs at the top end of the game. The atmosphere was great and everyone pulled together for the good of the club, from the office girl to the owner, Sam Hammam.

It was a family club and I loved every minute. There is a tradition at Wimbledon that every new player has to undergo a kind of initiation ceremony. I remember the stunt they pulled on me, and I suppose I got off lightly. When we hit the road for my first away match, they took the opportunity to rearrange my hotel room, and everything in it. I found clothing and kit in some very unusual places and it took me the best part of an hour to collect everything up and put it back in the right place. It was quite a genteel initiation compared to some I have seen, where players have had their jackets, shirts, ties and shoes all cut to pieces. At other times, players have been left stranded, naked, at the training ground! Others have had their tyres let down, or removed completely. Not one, but often three or four. One missing tyre is fairly easy to cope with, if you have a spare in the boot, but three or four becomes a problem. But all the pranks were done to generate team spirit. If players couldn't handle it, they had tricks played on them over and over again until they could.

The set-up at Wimbledon was very different from the City Ground. A much smaller club than Forest, their home ground at Plough Lane was a real dump. I couldn't believe it when I first saw it. Amateur clubs back home in Holland had much better facilities. And the crowds were pathetically low.

So why join them? Well, I wanted first-team football, they were in the First Division (now the Premiership, of course) and I liked Bobby Gould. He was a good manager, an excellent motivator with sound tactical knowledge. Bobby also had the respect of the players. You talked to him like he was one of the lads, unlike Cloughie! And the club's organization was actually vastly superior to Forest. Training was a lot harder and tactics were discussed on a much more advanced level. The system was completely different.

Above all, there was the camaraderie of the club. A great spirit ran through the whole set-up and I loved it. A classic essence of the Wimbledon approach at that time was the ghetto blaster we took into the changing-room before matches. The louder the music, the more we got psyched up before games. Now, it seems, every club uses one.

The most disappointing aspect of playing for the Dons was the crowds. Things got even worse when the club started to ground-share with Crystal Palace. For some cup games, played at home, only two or three thousand people would turn up at Selhurst Park. That's one reason why we loved to play away. There would always be big crowds and they booed us on and off the pitch. But coping with that kind of reaction has always been one of Wimbledon's strengths. The more stick we got, the more we loved it. The newspapers and the rest of the media always seemed to be against us, and that just helped to motivate us even more to prove people wrong.

Generally, we were all in favour of the move to Selhurst Park, a more modern and spacious stadium than Plough Lane. With Crystal Palace then playing in the Second Division, we felt it was our own ground, and a more suitable venue for top-class football. However, there were two drawbacks: the first was the journey to Palace – the traffic around that part of south London can be really awful. Secondly, clubs came to Palace thinking, 'This is a nice ground, with a big pitch, we can play here. Not like the dump at Plough Lane.' That was a drab old ground, with dirty changing-rooms and filthy showers, and none of the polished marble floors that greet you at some clubs. Teams visiting Wimbledon for the first time must have felt, 'What the hell are we doing here?' Most of them were 1–0 down before they started. Looking back, the place was a disgrace, but it was the place where we had our best times.

As I've said, the team spirit we had at Wimbledon was incredible. And we loved the chance of not only rubbing our shoulders with the big boys but rubbing their noses in the mud. When we went out onto the pitch, we felt we could beat anybody. It was a classic London mixture of cockiness and confidence. We worked well together, trained well together and played well together. The camaraderie was magnificent. There's only so much that coaching and preparation can do for you. That feeling of going out onto the pitch totally determined that you won't get beaten is impossible to pick up from a coaching manual.

In the first two or three seasons at Wimbledon we developed a saying: 'We came, we scored, we went.' That was it. When we played away, that was all we were interested in achieving. We felt that if we scored once, that would be enough for a draw at least. We won a lot of matches 1–0 and simply loved frustrating the big clubs. It was always something special to go to the big homes of the major clubs and get a result. They hated us and our long-ball football. But here we were, an upstart club who had moved to the top division from non-league football in such a short space of time, and the thing they hated most was the fact that they had to give us respect.

If someone like Glenn Hoddle played a forty-yard pass for a striker to run onto and score, it would be labelled beautiful, Brazilian-style football. When Vinnie Jones or Keith Curle knocked the ball forward for Big Fash to get hold of and score, it would be labelled 'route one' football. Double standards indeed.

Wimbledon always had a great record against Liverpool, especially after that famous FA Cup Final win at Wembley when my predecessor in goal, Dave Beasant, saved a penalty from John Aldridge. I just loved playing at Liverpool. The supporters are the best in the country and they even give the opposing goalkeepers a warm reception, especially at the Kop end. The atmosphere has changed quite a bit now that it's an all-seater stadium, and it seems a lot less noisy, but it's still an incredible place. Part of English footballing folklore.

My all-time favourite match for Wimbledon was at home to Liverpool on 14 December 1993 in the Coca-Cola Cup. We drew 2–2 and won the tie 4–3 on penalties to go through to the quarter-finals. We should have won it in normal time but Liverpool scored an amazing equalizer. Or, rather, I did. With a minute to go, Steve Nicol crossed the ball and I went out to catch it. I was under a lot of pressure, from Robbie Fowler if I remember correctly, and I punched the ball into my own net. That took the game into extra time and Liverpool had a great chance to win the tie when they were awarded a penalty, but I managed to save the spot kick from John Barnes. Then in the penalty shoot-out, I saved two more, from Mark Walters and Jamie Redknapp. It was definitely the most memorable match of my career and the club presented me with the match ball – for saving a hat-trick of penalties! Unfortunately, in the quarter-finals we were unable to reproduce that kind of battling performance and lost 2–1 at home to Sheffield Wednesday. It was so disappointing to play so badly at home. Maybe we would have been more fired up before a full house at Hillsborough.

I gained quite a reputation for saving penalties in my first years with the club. I stopped one from Aston Villa's Allan Evans when we won 1–0 away in the FA Cup, and saved another away to Everton in the quarter-finals, this one taken by Graeme Sharp, but we still lost 1–0. I also kept out one from Neil Ruddock in a 0–0 draw against Southampton.

At Wimbledon we always celebrated victory in a special way.

The Lebanese managing director and Nigerian-born centre forward would lead the Dutch goalkeeper and the rest of the squad, including several Jamaicans, in a good old Cockney-style sing-song. Everyone would join in, including Stanley Reed, then the chairman. He was a legend at the club and an incredibly fit man for his age. After matches, the players would stay behind for a few drinks and then climb aboard the coach, where Sam and Joe Kinnear, who had followed Bobby Gould, Ray Harford and Peter Withe as manager, would again be leading the singing, taking the mickey out of the players in just the same way as we took the mickey out of each other.

It was a brilliant time in my life and I really miss it. It was great to go back there with Wolves for an FA Cup tie. Sadly, I was injured and wasn't even able to make the bench. But it was good to see all the lads and the staff. Playing for Wimbledon was something very special.

As a family, we settled quite quickly into our new home on a pleasant estate in Fleet. It was quite a contrast. The standard of living in the south may be better, but people do like to live life at 100 miles an hour. I only see our neighbours at weekends or on long evenings in the summer. They are always working or travelling, a bit different from Nottingham, where life was more homely. But the most important thing was that Astrid settled down here, and our children were happy and contented with their friends and with school life.

However, that picture of domestic bliss was soon to be shattered.

5

THE SUN STING

That knock on the door by Hampshire Police certainly turned my world upside down for two and a half long years. It was hell for all of those involved and I thank God that justice was done and I still have my liberty.

I first heard about the whole business one day in November 1994 when I was returning home from a trip with a business partner, Alfonsus Thuys. We were producing individually designed ties for sports clubs and I remember receiving a phone call from Tony Stenson, a sports journalist on the *Daily Mirror*. He told me that another newspaper, presumably *The Sun*, was planning a big piece about footballers taking bribes to fix the results of matches. He asked me if I knew anything about it (presumably it was a slanted question to see if I was in any way involved) and I said, 'You must be having a laugh.' He said he was phoning every Premier league goalkeeper to get some feedback. Then, later on, another newspaper phoned with the same story, asking the same questions. The Fleet Street rumour mill was obviously working overtime.

By then, I had become involved in a little sideline, helping a Malaysian acquaintance, Richard Lim (real name Heng Suan Lim), to forecast the results of matches back home in Holland. He said the information was being used by clients in Malaysia and Indonesia. I could see nothing wrong in it. It was no different from inviting famous footballers on the TV every Saturday lunchtime to give their opinions on matches taking place that particular weekend.

Because of the press calls I had received, I phoned Sam Hammam, the Wimbledon owner, and told him what had happened. I told him that a couple of reporters had been on, accusing goalkeepers of taking bribes. I wasn't sure if my name was going to be mentioned or not. If it was, I told him that what they might be planning to print in the newspapers was not true and he told me not to worry. Sam's reaction was very positive and reassuring, and I felt a little more comfortable. He had been on the receiving end of a lot of fantasy journalism himself and was convinced that the stories were being fabricated. Later that night Tony Stenson called back and apologized for his earlier remarks, and said that it was the former Liverpool goalkeeper, Bruce Grobbelaar, now with Southampton, who was going to be splashed all over the papers the next day.

The following morning I picked up a copy of *The Sun* from the local newsagents and saw all the allegations about him receiving £2,000 from his business partner and so-called friend Chris Vincent in return for a promise to fix the results of matches. *The Sun* had got themselves involved in a blatant piece of entrapment, encouraging Vincent to hand sums of money to Bruce while their meeting was being filmed by a hidden camera in a hotel room in Southampton. I later learned that they had to set up the meeting twice, and go through the whole charade a second time, as, when they tried to do it the first time, Vincent was so drunk he forgot how to make the camera work. *The Sun* had called in a specialist team of investigative journalists to bug the room, and the results were hazy and inconclusive.

Later that evening, one or two reporters called me for my reaction to the story and I told them it seemed like a huge con-trick that had gone wrong. When the topic was discussed at training earlier that day, the players all felt that Bruce had been set up. A lot of professional footballers get involved in business dealings outside the game and you like to think you can trust the people you are working with. They felt disgusted that a man like Vincent should try to destroy Bruce with these incredible allegations. I heard nothing more about it until that knock on the door on the Tuesday morning the following March.

Then all hell broke loose. Just try to put yourself in my shoes for a moment and imagine this scenario if you can. You are a professional footballer, enjoying life in the Premier League. You are a happily married family man, with a nice house, a beautiful wife and two gorgeous children. Everything in your life seems to be turning out the way you would want it to.

Then, suddenly, your world explodes. The police knock on your door first thing in the morning with a search warrant to go through the house. The press have been tipped off and a group of photographers and TV cameramen are waiting outside the house.

Ironically, the neighbours who witnessed these fantastic scenes thought it was because I had had a bust-up with the Wimbledon manager, Joe Kinnear. Just to fill in a little detail, a week before the arrest I had spoken to Joe about our reserve goalkeeper, Neil Sullivan. His contract was up and Joe was not sure what to do. He asked me if I would mind if Neil played a few first team matches to put him in the shop window and hopefully attract some offers from other clubs. Joe wanted to see how Neil reacted to playing in the first team, and to see if he could handle the pressure of Premier League football.

For a small club like Wimbledon, without a ground of their own and operating on a shoestring budget because of their pitifully small crowds, selling players was an important lifeline to bring in valuable revenue. There was no disagreement between Joe and me, quite the opposite, even though it did affect my wages at Wimbledon. At that time I was on a bonus of £500 whenever I kept a clean sheet.

As I've said, Wimbledon was like a big, happy family. And I was part of the furniture, part of that family. I would do anything to help the club, so standing aside for a while to let Neil in between the posts was not a problem. Actually, Neil did really well and in his first match, away to Sheffield Wednesday, we won 1-0. I don't know if he was on the same sort of bonus arrangement as me.

One week later, I was arrested. And until the end of the season, I stayed on the bench while Neil stayed in goal. The club were convinced of my innocence and wanted to help me as much as they could. They wanted to protect me from the pressure I was under, and with the criminal proceedings going on and all sorts of things being said, they thought it might be better if I stayed on the bench.

Being arrested in your own home is not a pleasant experience, I can assure you. The police read out the charges, explained my rights and told me they were taking me to Eastleigh police station, near Southampton. They said I was being charged with attempting to defraud bookmakers. During the journey, I was accompanied by two other officers, one driving and a female officer sat next to the driver. I was stuck in the back seat on my own. They were both quite civil and courteous, I suppose, although conversation was minimal. Mostly, I asked them questions concerning how long I would be needed and what time could I expect to get home again later in the day.

When we arrived at Eastleigh police station around 10am, there were more teams of photographers waiting outside. I expected to go into a room of some kind to answer questions, and I wasn't prepared for the shock that was in store. I was shown straight to a cell and the door slammed shut behind me.

It was a small police station, very drab and very cold. And I was in a cell. I couldn't believe it. You see these images on films and on television and you see people like murderers and rapists locked up, but you never imagine that you are ever going to end up inside one yourself. I was left there for one and a half hours.

When it came to my first interview with the police, I was shown into a tiny room and I sat in a chair in the corner. There were two officers on the other side of the room. One of them read me my rights and, as I was beginning to take all this in, they started to bombard me with questions from left, right and centre. Again you see scenes like this on television, in programmes like *The Bill*, but you never imagine what it is going to be like in real life. If you have never been in trouble with the police before, it is all new and frightening.

During the first interview it was obvious that they were trying to make me feel uncomfortable. They would raise their voices, then lower them, all the time trying to intimidate and unnerve me. They pretended to know more than they did and tried to unsettle me with their tactics.

We had a break for lunch and I was taken back to the cell. I was offered a coffee, which tasted like dishwater. Then came lunch. It was scrambled eggs and baked beans served up on a tinfoil plate, heated up in the oven. The police officer who acted as a waiter apologized for the quality of the food.

The second interview seemed go on for hours. I thought they were never going to stop. All sorts of feelings and fears were going through my mind. Had I simply said nothing, then everything would have been OK. But the more I said, the more questions they asked.

Looking back, the police tactics were simple. They made out they knew the lot but in fact they knew very little. The only thing they knew was that I had had contact with John Fashanu and Richard Lim. They were trotting things out, things that had nothing to do with the case at all. All the time they were trying to trip me up, trying to put words into my mouth, trying to say things that would trap me into incriminating myself. They even suggested that I had received death threats to comply with the wishes of this so-called gambling syndicate they said was operating in the Far East.

I had thought that my giving advice to Richard Lim was all perfectly acceptable and harmless. Unfortunately, I had not checked FA regulations, which state that players and football officials are not allowed to be involved in assisting with any form of gambling on matches. I knew that I had done nothing illegal, but now I feared that I could be in big trouble with the FA.

Eventually, I cracked. I don't know why I said it, to this day, but to steer them away from football matters, I made up some story about stealing cars when I was a kid in Holland and that was where the money they were quizzing me about had come from. It was the first time they had had a smile on their faces since I had met them earlier that day. When I saw them laughing, it was fairly obvious that they did not believe me. Quite rightly, they called it a fairy story.

I was stunned when the police insisted that I remain in custody overnight. I was allowed to telephone Astrid to tell her the news. She was crying. The cell was miserable and cold and I remember keeping my overcoat on as I tried in vain to get some sleep. I felt dirty, hungry, and lost several pounds in weight during this ordeal. The most humiliating part was having to pose for the police photographs. I am sure it's done just to make you feel like a criminal.

The detectives taped everything that was said and after a third interview the following day, I had four forms to sign. At this point I felt it was time to see a lawyer. A local solicitor, Mr Peach, appeared and sat down with me in the cell. He told me I had said far too much already and not to say any more after this.

Mr Peach arranged bail and later I learned that Mel Goldberg had phoned Astrid after hearing the news of my arrest on his car radio and asked why we had not called him in to help. To be honest, I had only thought of Mel as a sports lawyer and did not realize that he was qualified to deal in criminal cases as well.

While at Eastleigh, I realized that Richard Lim was also in custody. I recognized his shoes outside a cell door. The food may have been awful, but the overnight shoeshine service was obviously a lot better! I wondered what was happening to Richard and whether he, like me a foreigner here and a stranger to the English legal system, had been undergoing the same harrowing ordeal as I had.

While I was in custody I was allowed to telephone Astrid at home and received more orders to speak in English and not in

Dutch. That was ridiculous, because Astrid and I always speak Dutch to each other when we are together. I felt so small because someone was bullying me into speaking their language and not mine. I assured Astrid that everything would be fine.

After thirty-six hours in that cell it was a joy to breathe the fresh air and get home to my family. But that wasn't the end of the matter. It was the beginning.

Once I had got home, I received a phone call from my church minister. He was in charge when I was doing my Alpha course, which is an introduction to Christianity. The call was very encouraging and we prayed together on the telephone, for Astrid, the children and myself. But deep inside I felt really depressed. Never before in my life had the spotlight been on me in this way and I found it very difficult to cope with. I imagine most people would feel the same way. After I was released the media chased me non-stop and at one stage, to avoid the photographers, Astrid and I would arrange to meet at secret locations.

Our home was surrounded and Astrid complained that every time she went out of the house she was ambushed by photographers. I was extremely worried about her and the children. In some ways you get used to the attention through being a professional footballer, although not on this scale. But Astrid and the children had had no experience of it at all, and I was worried about how they would react to such horrendous pressure. Even the Dutch media came over and camped out on our doorstep. They wanted to know everything about the case and so I invited them inside for a short interview. I told them the background to the case, but I couldn't tell them too much detail because by now the legal wheels were in motion and people had to wait until the trial for everything to come out into the open. It was a problem sitting on the truth until the trial started, but I knew that when the truth came out people would know we were innocent.

Astrid and I talked for hours and days on end about the case and the position we found ourselves in. We wondered what would be the response from the media, and we worried about the reaction from our family and friends in Holland. The initial reports were shocking. Our family and friends back home were devastated. Even relatives in Australia saw the news beamed at them from their TV set.

The day after I had been released from custody, I tried to get hold of John Fashanu. I rang his number on several occasions but learned that he was in hiding, trying to escape from the media pressure. Eventually, two days later, we met up in his London office to talk things through. We were both really down and neither one of us could believe what was happening. We both felt the whole world was going mad. His family had seen the news on TV in Nigeria and were equally distraught. It was difficult to keep things in perspective and Fash said we had to be strong and deal with it together.

I also spoke to Richard Lim and he told me that the story had made big headlines in Indonesia and Malaysia. Richard was very laid-back but again said he could not believe the things that were happening. Richard echoed many of the words Fash had said. He felt it was important for us to stick together as a team and to make sure we had a good team behind us.

Looking back on things, the reaction from friends and neighbours was astonishing. They were the best friends you could have wished for – no matter how bad the publicity was, their loyalty towards us never wavered. They helped to look after the children when we had to attend meetings and were always there to offer comfort and support if we needed it.

You don't realize how close and loving people can be until you are faced with such a monumental crisis. The good thing about it was that they knew nothing about the case and did not dream of asking any awkward or embarrassing questions. They knew us, trusted us and cared for us, and unless you are in a situation like that, you have no idea just how comforting it is to have such people around you.

6

ANYBODY GOT A SPARE KNEE?

As the case progressed, I sensed a change in the mood towards me at Wimbledon. The club were always very understanding and I did my best to keep them fully in the picture about developments in the case, but I have to say that Sam Hammam was not the Sam I knew. With all the questions being raised about my integrity and honesty, perhaps it was understandable that some of those doubts started surfacing in the minds of people at Wimbledon. You know what they say, throw a lot of mud and some of it sticks.

But Joe Kinnear, the manager, was always loyal and supportive. We had numerous discussions about the case during this period and he offered to help me in any way possible. 'You just have to ask,' he said. What a great guy and a great manager. He was there for me on the field and off it.

As for the Crazy Gang, there was all sorts of stick and mickey-taking right up until I left the club, but it was what I expected. The banter and the merciless ribbing is quite normal in the football world. If you can't handle it, then it is best that you look elsewhere for your employment.

The phone calls were non-stop. Not so much from the other Wimbledon players, because I would see them every day at training, but from people I didn't even know, usually just wishing me well and in some cases to say they were praying for me. That was something very special.

Amidst everything else, I still had to concentrate on my football. As I mentioned, I spent the rest of that season on the bench for Wimbledon. In the summer, I resumed pre-season training and was struggling with a knee injury. We went on a training camp to a Navy base near Plymouth and after a lot of fitness work, we played two games against local teams. I was comfortable with all aspects of my goalkeeping apart from one: kicking. As most fans will know, that is a vital part of the game if you are keeping goal for a team like Wimbledon, who have perfected the art of fast, direct counter-attacking. It may not always be pretty but it is certainly effective. In Brian Clough's words, it is all about keeping the game simple. In business terms, you are cutting out the middle man. In football terms, it means you sometimes cut out the midfield.

I must admit I felt uncomfortable with my kicking and the medical staff decided the knee needed looking at. I rested the knee until August, when I went into hospital for an exploratory operation. I came back in October and played a couple of reserve games, but the knee started swelling up again after matches and training. The medical staff had a basic remedy for this. They would insert a syringe into my knee and use it to remove the fluid building up around the kneecap. This would either take place at the training ground or at the doctor's surgery. It was done without anaesthetic. And I can tell you, it is one of the most painful things you could ever imagine.

The treatment helped but after one or two days the swelling returned after training and it was obvious that the knee was not 100 per cent right. I underwent another operation in London in October, at the Wellington Hospital in St John's Wood. This time the knee felt a lot better afterwards and I was ready to return to action in December. The club were certainly looking to get me back on the pitch as soon as possible, because we were struggling close to the relegation zone and they wanted more experience at the back.

My first match back with the first team was on Boxing Day away to Chelsea. We won 2-1 at Stamford Bridge and I stayed in the side for the next two games. Two or three days later we had another London derby match, this time away to Arsenal, and we won again, this time 3-1. On New Year's Day we faced Everton at home and, on a mudbath of a pitch, lost 3-2. During the match I felt my knee go again, and later in the evening it started to swell up.

This kept me out of the early New Year games and I was booked in for yet another operation in January. By that time I had got so fed up with the surgeon that I demanded to go somewhere else. We had thought it was a cartilage problem but when my knee was opened up a third time, they discovered pieces of tissue flocking together on the bone. This time they had to shave them off and drill two holes in the bone to encourage new tissue to grow again. I have always wondered why this condition was not discovered during the first two operations. Apparently this type of problem does not always show up on an X-ray and the only way they can detect it is by opening up the knee. If anyone tries to tell you that being a professional footballer is an easy life, then I would happily allow them to swap my place on the treatment table when someone is opening up your knee.

While I was out of action and recovering from the third operation, Neil Sullivan came back into the side and stayed in until the end of the season. Wimbledon, in the meantime, had also signed another promising goalkeeper, Paul Heald from Leyton Orient. Paul quickly showed he had the ability to jump from the bottom division to the top and was a very good shot-stopper.

At the end of the season, I was released by Wimbledon, perhaps not surprisingly. They now had two other goalkeepers on the staff and I had the problem with my knee, as well the little matter of a court case to attend to. But it did not take me long to find another job. Once again, another player was able to help me get fixed up with a new club. Keith Curle, who had played with me for three years at Wimbledon, was still a good friend. He had gone from Wimbledon to Manchester City and then on to Wolverhampton Wanderers. At Wimbledon he and I had always travelled together for training. We played golf, our families socialized and we were room-mates for away games.

Keith had just joined Wolves from City and I phoned him and asked what the situation was at Molineux. Wolves are a club with a fantastic pedigree, a rich and famous history and a fabulous stadium, but were struggling to win back what they thought was their rightful place in the Premiership. Keith spoke on my behalf to the manager, Mark McGhee, who invited me up to the Midlands for a chat. Naturally, he wanted to know all about the case, how things were going and how confident we were of getting through it all. I told him that we had everything under control and we were just waiting for the right result.

He was quite happy with the answers I had given him and so on the following Monday afternoon, I played for Wolves reserves against Leicester City reserves at Molineux. We won 3–0 but it was the most nerve-racking experience I have ever faced on a football field. I knew I had to do well. Being in a situation like that, I was aware that it might not be easy to find another club willing to take me on with the court case hanging over my head. Luckily, Mark McGhee and Wolves had confidence in me and were willing to let me play. I played for them throughout the trial on a non-contract basis. But I was delighted simply to be involved in football still while all sorts of legal mayhem was going on around me.

It was to be twenty months before I made my full debut for Wolves, but there was plenty to think about in the meantime.

7

PREPARING FOR THE TRIAL

As the court case grew nearer, I was involved in numerous meetings with my solicitor, Mel Goldberg. The meetings took place in legal offices, or 'chambers', at the Inns of Court in central London. The halls all look the same and it is a place where it is easy to get lost. During the early meetings, we discussed the charges against me and how I was going to plead. Obviously, for me there was only one answer: not guilty.

Mel then introduced me to a barrister, Desmond de Silva QC, and his junior Stephen Berrick. Desmond said that he would be willing to handle the case and explained how the legal procedure would work and how my defence strategy would develop. After that meeting, I felt good about what they had said in my favour and I phoned Mel later to confirm that I would like them as my defence team.

The period leading up to the case was hard work, just like commuting up to London all the time for meetings. Every time we met, Mel had been presented with new evidence which he then discussed with me.

It seems crazy now, but I must admit I was a bit lazy about things early on. I suppose I just didn't realize how serious the whole thing was, but after the pre-trial hearings in court I began to realize the weight of the charges. There was so much publicity in the newspapers, which we felt was obviously prejudicial, that we hoped the trial would be thrown out before it started. During our meetings I made brief notes to check things when I got home, such as personal financial details, bank details, phone calls, and dates of certain football matches in England and in Holland.

By now, the charges against Melissa, John Fashanu's wife, had been dropped. So the four people left facing charges were John, Bruce Grobbelaar, Richard Lim and myself. We were all facing charges individually but the trials were all due to take place at the same time, with the four of us sitting side by side in the dock. This meant we all had separate defence teams.

I already had a good relationship with Fash because we were Wimbledon team-mates, and as the case developed this relationship became very special. He had helped me with my business activities and had introduced me to Richard Lim, a real football fanatic with a brilliant sense of humour.

I first met Richard, through Fash, in the summer of 1993. Richard explained about his forecasting business and his friends in Malaysia who were gambling on the results of Dutch matches. He wondered if I could help him with that project and when he discussed the money involved, it felt like Christmas coming early. Plus a good bonus now and again, just for talking about football. In the beginning, we would see each other at least once a week for a couple of hours to talk about forecasts and about football in general. He was full of it. He knew more about what was happening in English football than I did. Richard was a great guy.

The more I thought about it, the more difficult I realized it was to accurately forecast matches. So I bought a decoder which meant I could tune in to Dutch TV to keep up with the football news from back home. That extra information would help me with the forecasting.

I still keep in touch with Richard, especially after the ordeal of going through two trials lasting five to six months. When you see each other every day, as we did at Winchester, you develop a special relationship. Richard is slowly getting his life back together and is in the process of starting a new business. A few months after the second trial, his wife gave birth to a lovely baby daughter, so he is now a very proud father.

Initially, as we prepared for the trial, I was advised to be very careful about getting too close to the other defendants because although we were on trial together, there would be individual verdicts. So every man was on his own . . .

All sorts of thoughts went through my mind. Did I have the wrong defence team? I had serious doubts about things at one stage and prayed to the Lord for guidance. I had received calls from one or two friends in football saying that Mel was not a criminal lawyer and not the right man to do the job. They said I needed a specialist criminal solicitor.

Two days later, Mel called and told us that Desmond had invited us for a working lunch at his exclusive club. It was a very posh place and potentially intimidating. But Desmond is such a wonderful man that he soon defused any fears we had and after the meeting we went away feeling reassured about the direction of the case. And I was sure that we had the right people after all. I drove back to Fleet and thanked the Lord. The defence teams felt the same way as I did. Everybody started working well with each other and things went from strength to strength. Looking back, I realize that I underestimated Mel's abilities. He and Jan Cook, his assistant, worked day and night on the case to get me ready for the battle ahead.

The teams representing John, Richard and me all began corresponding with each other and arranged several meetings together where we would discuss any new evidence that came along and how it should be dealt with. Bruce Grobbelaar's defence team were based in the north, so we met only a few times. When Bruce and I spoke, he always struck me as being a supremely confident man. During the trial we got to know each other a lot better and became very close. We kept encouraging each other and shared a lot of laughter and tears. We gave each other a shoulder to cry on.

The approach to the trial was a bit like an extended pre-season. During the build-up the spirit in my camp was good, with a lot of simple yet positive advice and no little humour. Every time we went to court for a committal hearing I hoped that the case would get thrown out there and then, but my team always knew it would go all the way.

There were highs and lows along the way. The highs were the reassuring messages of support from so many people, good friends and strangers alike, and the lows were facing the media and sitting in court, listening to the arguments.

I received lots of letters from Wimbledon supporters saying they felt I was totally innocent and that they didn't believe anything they had read in the papers. It was very encouraging to find out that the club's supporters were standing by me. I had always had a good relationship with them and it was such a shame that the club did not have a bigger following to help them compete with the big boys. I received good luck cards from fans and letters of support from people we hardly knew. Business contacts from the tie firm were also very supportive. I received such a great psychological lift from these people and still appreciate the help they gave so freely and so warmly.

There were a few crank calls on the answerphone, with songs and rude comments, and once I received an envelope containing a piece of toilet paper and you can guess what else was inside. I never told Astrid about these things – I thought she might get scared. You never know what people might get up to.

Then the date was set for 14 January 1997 at Winchester Crown Court. It seemed a long way away at the time but the people around me warned that it would go quickly. They were right. I had to get ready, to be prepared to fight for my livelihood and my freedom.

During the first trial, when I entered the witness box to give evidence and be questioned by Desmond, he forgot two of my Christian names and said: 'Are you Hans Johannes Segers?'

I said: 'No.'

He quipped: 'Then I have been representing the wrong man all this time!'

The courtroom echoed with laughter as I reminded Desmond of my full name. It would have been nice to have said: 'That's it – they've obviously got the wrong man. Maybe I can go now.'

Both trials were marathon affairs. The Crown Prosecution Service (CPS) was bringing charges against four individuals, but we were being tried together because they alleged it was a conspiracy.

They produced the video evidence manufactured by *The Sun* and Chris Vincent, to try to incriminate Bruce. Then they produced lists of telephone calls made between the defendants, although they admitted that there had been no calls between Bruce and myself. Nor should there have been. We had played against each other several times, but the only time I had met him, apart from on the football field, was at a charity golf day.

There were plenty of good reasons, however, for me talking to Fash on the telephone. He was a team-mate, a good friend and we were planning a couple of property ventures in London. I also confirmed that I often spoke to Richard about Dutch football matches.

The CPS produced lists of payments made into my bank, which were from the ties business, fees from Richard for forecasting, and sums from Fash towards the property deals. As Fash was often out of the country, it made sense for me to have the cash in my bank just in case we needed to make a quick payment for something.

The Crown also had access to lists of telephone calls between Fash, Richard, and Richard's business contacts in Malaysia and Indonesia.

Richard's friends were extremely wealthy people who loved to have a bet. But there was nothing illegal in that. The prosecution tried to make out that it was something huge, something sinister. They pretended it was something to do with a big syndicate. They exaggerated everything to build up a picture for the jury. But the truth was very different. It was just a handful of incredibly wealthy people having a flutter. People can't imagine how much money these guys spend. Often they would stake bets worth £20,000 with each other, whereas the normal guy in the street might spend only £5 in a betting shop.

During the first trial, the prosecution showed video highlights of nineteen Wimbledon matches I had played in. The one they highlighted was that famous 3–2 defeat at Everton on the last day of the 1993–4 season. Everton had to win to stay up and there was tremendous pressure on them. But as usual, we loved nothing better than going away to a big stadium with a packed house roaring on the home team. We soaked up everything they threw at us in the first half and twice hit them on the break to go 2–0 up. Suddenly we were all over them and it looked like they were heading for relegation.

After half-time they pulled a goal back through a penalty, and then Barry Horne struck an absolute screamer from twenty-five yards that flew past me into the top corner. And as everybody knows, they then grabbed a winning goal. Graham Stuart was on the edge of the box, maybe just inside it, when he hit a shot that took a deflection off another player's leg, so that made the ball change direction slightly. The pitch was uneven, as you would expect at the end of the season, and the ball hit a bump and spun beyond my control as I dived. The goal saved them from relegation and Sheffield United went down instead.

Looking at the videos it was obvious to anyone who knows about football that I was making a genuine attempt to save that shot from Stuart. Having studied that video at least twenty times you detect little things and I noticed that my standing leg gave way very slightly, probably because of the state of the pitch. I was diving to my right expecting to save the shot and the ball hit that bump and just popped over my hand. Yes, I felt sick. All goalkeepers do when they let in a goal in such circumstances. But take a look at the past couple of seasons. You will have seen similar goals go in against England goalkeepers Tim Flowers and Ian Walker, when shots that should have been comfortably saved have hit a divot. No one would accuse them of letting the ball in deliberately. But that's the accusation I had to face.

As a goalkeeper you expect to save those kinds of shot and you are absolutely disgusted with yourself when they go in. Of the nineteen videos produced by the prosecution, that was the only mistake they pinpointed. Nothing else emerged apart from that one dodgy bounce, and that was why the prosecution threw their weight behind that one goal.

From my point of view, the charges against me were always very suspect. The police started off trying to accuse me of attempting to defraud bookmakers. Then the charge switched to conspiracy. Then, in the first trial, they accused me of throwing matches. In the second trial, that accusation switched to trying to influence results. All the time their case was getting weaker and they changed their tactics to suit themselves. In the end it was obvious that they would have had no case at all but for the fact that I had made up some crazy stories in that police cell.

During the trial, I managed to keep fit by training at Woking, the ambitious Vauxhall Conference club whose excellent ground was about twenty minutes' drive from home. I called Geoff Chapple, their manager, and he was happy for me to train with them on Tuesday and Thursday evenings.

I actually played for them once to help them out in an FA Trophy tie away to Dorchester when their regular goalkeeper had injured his hand. This was in the middle of the first trial and not surprisingly I received a lot of stick from Dorchester fans behind the goal. The match was being shown on Sky TV and the fans were chanting stuff like, 'You're going down with Grobbelaar.'

It was 1-1 in the second half when I rushed out of my goal for a one-on-one situation with their striker. We collided and the referee awarded Dorchester a penalty. I felt I had gone for the ball and it was an instinctive goalkeeper's reaction to argue with the decision. Anyway, I saved the penalty but they scored from the rebound.

Although Woking were a non-league club they were good to me and I was really psyched up for the game and wanted to do well for them. We scored ten minutes from time to equalize at 2-2 and

I turned round and raised my fist towards the fans who had been giving me so much verbal abuse. It was a visual way of saying, 'up yours', but the fans went wild and a policeman marched on to the pitch, put his face in mine and said, 'I am going to report you.' I told him not to bother because I was in enough trouble already at Winchester. Anyway, he left it like that and then we scored in the dying seconds to snatch a 3–2 win. Again I faced a volley of abuse as I left the pitch, but it was a huge relief to get a result in such a hostile atmosphere. After the match I went to see the policeman, apologized to him and explained the situation I was involved in at Winchester. He hadn't realized who I was and he said sorry and we shook hands. He said they were not used to dealing with such big crowds at Dorchester and to forget about it.

That was the only match I played for Woking and I was happy to help them out. From a personal point of view I should never have played. I didn't really do myself justice. I wasn't match fit and lacked match practice, even at a lower level. They say that the Cup is a great leveller. It certainly was that day.

PART TWO

THE LAWYER'S STORY

By Mel Goldberg

1

THE CALL THAT NEVER CAME

SPORT and the law – those are the two areas that have dominated my working life for more than twenty years. I have managed world boxing champions, advised successful Premier League football clubs on commercial and legal affairs, and negotiated several multi-million pound transfer deals involving major international soccer stars. But, apart from the birth of my three children, nothing can compare for emotion with the football trial at Winchester Crown Court, where my client, Hans Segers, was one of the four defendants.

As the trial drew near, boxes stacked high with documents filled my office. Normally I can sit at my desk, in beautiful surroundings near Marble Arch, in the West End of London, and look out of the window over Hyde Park. However, when I moved from my desk to the window I ran the grave risk of tripping over boxes of evidence, information from the Crown Prosecution Service, plus meticulously filed witness statements. There were also several boxes full of videotapes of the matches which formed the basis of the Crown's claim that these famous, well-paid football stars had attempted to earn even more money by trying to influence the result of Premier League matches.

It was nonsense. It is surely difficult, if not impossible, to influence the outcome of a match between two teams of eleven players unless all twenty-two individuals, plus the referee and linesmen, are in collusion.

The legal arguments were fascinating. Because it was going to be a 'celebrity trial' involving international soccer stars, and therefore certain to generate huge amounts of publicity for the major legal players, my phone didn't stop ringing for weeks with solicitors and barristers all eager to gain a toehold on the case. Some phoned for a hint of inside information, others were desperate to get a job on one of the defence teams appointed individually by the four defendants. Invitations to drinks, lunches and dinners flowed fast and furious.

I first met Hans and Astrid Segers around 1992 when I was working in the City with a legal firm called Bird and Bird. Hans came to me as a client because he wanted me to negotiate a new contract for him at Wimbledon, which I duly did. Some five years later, the Crown Prosecution Service would go through that contract with a fine-tooth comb. I dealt with Wimbledon's chief executive officer, David Barnard, and after some hard bargaining got Hans what I thought was a very good deal. I also worked with Jo Kirran, who was a female football agent, and I used to conclude the contracts which she negotiated on Hans's behalf.

I first heard about the case against Bruce Grobbelaar in November 1994 when I read the coverage of *The Sun*'s infamous and incredible sting operation. I did not know Bruce Grobbelaar personally but I had a high regard for him as both an outstanding goalkeeper and a character. I remember thinking at the time that I could not believe those allegations were true.

There were no whispers about Hans's arrest before it was made, although between the date Bruce was first arrested and when Hans was ultimately arrested, I did hear a rumour that Hans was involved. I found that, too, impossible to believe.

I first learned of Hans's arrest when I received a call from Jo Kirran. She phoned in a panic at around 10am on the day Hans was arrested and told me she had read about it on Teletext. I phoned Hans's house but got no answer. I was shocked by news of the arrest and desperately tried to get hold of Hans because I knew that he needed help. But I could not get through either on the telephone landline or on his mobile. I was in the office at the time and so I could not check the TV and Teletext, but I spoke to some friends of mine in the press and they confirmed the arrest. For two whole days I tried unsuccessfully to get through to him.

It was not until around noon the following day that I managed to speak to Astrid. She was absolutely distraught about the whole business, but was at least relieved that Hans was being allowed home. She had known nothing about any of the alleged activities and it came as a dreadful shock to her.

Hans eventually telephoned me to say that he had been released. Not asking for me at the time of the arrest was a big mistake, but later he told me it was because he thought he had done nothing wrong and therefore could answer any questions without the help of a solicitor.

As is often the situation, a major part of the case against Hans was the interview in the police station in my absence, all of which was taken down and used in evidence against him at the trial. He asked for the duty solicitor only on the second day when he was requested to sign some authorities of disclosure to the bank and to the Inland Revenue, giving his permission for the police and tax authorities to investigate his financial affairs.

By then, of course, it was too late and much damage had been done. It was only after the questioning had been completed that the duty solicitor arrived. By that time, everything that Hans had said had been recorded. At a later date I heard the interview on tape and understood the kind of pressure that the police had put him under. Subsequently, every time he met the police for interviews I was with him, but because of the statements he had made to the police in the first interview without me, it was always a case of damage limitation.

The ordeal was so overwhelming for Hans that he lost between eight and ten pounds in weight in the space of a few days. I said to Astrid that when he felt better perhaps they should come and see me at the office. At that stage, Hans had not been charged.

Some weeks later, he and Astrid came to see me in London. Hans came to my office and started to give me the details. He told me he lied because he was worried about a possible breach of FA rules, namely forecasting, which assisted others in betting. He was worried about an FA ban. Hans was asked to attend Eastleigh police station for further questioning and I arranged to go with him. I travelled to Eastleigh by train and Hans collected me from the railway station and drove me to the police station. As we approached the building, we were surrounded by a horde of photographers, TV cameramen and reporters. It was a scene we were to get used to as the months went by. There was huge international media interest because of the backgrounds of the defendants: Hans from Holland, Bruce Grobbelaar from Zimbabwe, Richard Lim from Malaysia and John Fashanu with his African connections.

The police treated us pleasantly and Hans was interviewed by two officers in my presence. By then he felt much more comfort-able and answered all their questions as fully as he could. The interview lasted for about two hours and fortunately Hans did not repeat any of the unfortunate admissions (about cars) he had made during his first interviews. When any difficult questions arose, I intervened.

Some time later, we were asked to go back to Eastleigh police station. On our return, I said to the police that Hans had already answered their questions in some detail and that he did not want to answer any more questions. The police then said that if Hans did not answer any more questions, he could be charged. I said, 'So be it,' and every question that was then put to Hans was met with a curt reply: 'No comment.'

It was clear that the police had done a lot of investigating and they asked a number of questions that they had not asked before. They dealt with a lot of new areas of investigation, including the number of mobile telephone calls between various parties, and details of Hans's bank accounts. The detectives asked a barrage of questions to which I suspect they already knew, or thought they knew, the answers.

At the end of the interview, which was shorter than the previous one because we did not answer any questions in detail, they said they were going to charge Hans, together with others, of corruptly conspiring to defraud bookmakers. On behalf of Hans, I said that my client denied all charges and reserved his defence. If the matter came before a court, he would plead not guilty. They then charged him and subsequently took him off to another room to take his fingerprints and a mugshot for their files. That is all part of the degradation process. I felt very sad for Hans but he took it quite well. I had witnessed people being charged many times and it is never pleasant.

I later learned that Richard Lim, a Malaysian businessman, had been in the same police station at the same time. I did not see him, and at that stage would not have known him anyway. Later, we became quite friendly. I also learned that Bruce Grobbelaar and John Fashanu were at different police stations facing similar charges. Grobbelaar faced an additional charge in relation to alleg-edly accepting a sum of money from Chris Vincent which had been supplied by *The Sun* newspaper. That incident was shown repeatedly on national TV.

When we came out into the sunlight, we were met with the familiar barrage of cameras and questions. I gave a short denial on Hans's behalf to the press. The TV and radio news bulletins that day were full of the story, and so was Teletext. The next day every national newspaper carried headlines about the case.

At a later date I had meetings with Bruce Grobbelaar's solicitor, David Hewitt. I liked him from the outset and during the course of the trials struck up a close friendship. Ironically, he was an Everton supporter. Subsequently numerous meetings took place both with Hans and also with the other players and their respective legal teams. At that stage I had not been supplied with any evidence and only knew of the line of attack from the questioning being carried out by the police.

We then had to set about the task of choosing counsel – a barrister to put Hans's case in court. However, there was a hearing at Southampton magistrates' court where I represented Hans without counsel. It was there that I met Bruce Grobbelaar, John Fashanu and Richard Lim for the first time, although of course I had seen the first two in action on the football field on many occasions. The purpose of that hearing in Southampton was to formally charge the four individuals in court. When the charges were read out, the four all pleaded not guilty and the whole process was over in less than an hour.

Years before, I had advised John's brother, Justin Fashanu, when he was planning a transfer from Norwich City. Arsenal and Nottingham Forest were in competition for his signature. At that time Justin was the more famous of the two brothers and I remember him telling me that he was pleased to see that John had started to do well at Millwall and that the limelight would be shared by the two of them. I was trying to persuade Justin to move to Arsenal but after a day of negotiations, Brian Clough took him to one side and persuaded him to sign for Forest at three o'clock in the morning.

I don't know what Cloughie said but it did not turn out to be the dream move Justin had envisaged. The £1million transfer fee proved to be a huge millstone round his neck. After scoring the goal of the season for Norwich, Justin's career took a nosedive at Nottingham and never recovered. It was tragic to see that Justin died in such controversial circumstances in the spring of 1998. He was facing allegations of homosexual misconduct in America and hanged himself in a lock-up garage in the East End of London. John was deeply upset by his brother's death.

John was a different character from Justin, much tougher and with a great physical presence. As I got to know him, he proved to be extremely intelligent and was always immaculately dressed. He was charming to members of the public and never refused to sign autographs, going out of his way to speak to people in the street. Amazingly, John was not a great football fan himself and rarely discussed matches, but he loved training and working out and was especially formidable in the physical aspects of the game. He told me once that he had two or three black belts in martial arts, and that interested me because I had a brown and white belt in karate and, like John, I always worked out in the gym and used weights to keep fit. John came to a party of mine once and went round speaking to everybody. You could say he was the life and soul of the party and you could see why he was the ideal front man for Gladiators.

I always got on very well with his personal assistant, known to us all only as Mace, who was an ex-professional footballer and John's right-hand man. He always had a nice smile. John's solicitor, Henri Brandman, acted successfully for boxers Terry Marsh and Nigel Benn and is often to be seen in the West End of London at lunchtime, walking his poodle.

When the defendants met at court, they greeted each other like long-lost friends and there was a lot of hugging and back-slapping. They were to rely heavily on that kind of sporting bond when it came to boosting morale during the ordeal of two trials at Winchester. Fash, in particular, was always upbeat and smiling.

Again, the publicity was phenomenal. I had never seen so many reporters and photographers in one place at the same time. When you see film stars and the like being hounded by the press on TV it is one thing, but when you are caught up in the middle of it, and you see it as it really is, it is a different thing altogether. You begin to understand what it is like for a famous personality to have no privacy. Every member of the public feels entitled to speak to them as a matter of right. The players were persistently bombarded for autographs, even by individuals like the clerk of the court! They always obliged with a smile.

There were two or three further hearings in the magistrates' court, all of which I attended on Hans's behalf without counsel. I had decided to hire Desmond de Silva QC to lead our defence and I had two conferences with him and his junior counsel, Stephen Berrick. Desmond was one of the most impressive lawyers I had ever met. I admired him enormously and it was a privilege to work with him.

The structure of this relationship might be difficult for some to understand, so I will explain it as simply as I can. As a solicitor, I was employed by my client, Hans Segers. I then make recommendations to the client about which barrister, or counsel, to use to put the case in court. Usually clients know very little about the legal framework and rely on the expert advice of their solicitor.

I arranged a meeting for Hans to meet Desmond and Stephen. Stephen, as the junior counsel, prepares the case for the leading counsel. This usually entails a considerable amount of painstaking research. I knew Stephen from his sporting connections. During the trial he acquired the nickname of 'Cellsite One', because of the time he spent liaising with his office on his mobile phone.

Desmond de Silva, to borrow footballing parlance, is a megastar of the legal profession. His legal team have acted in some of the most high-profile cases in the land. As well as the football trial, members of his chambers featured prominently in the longest fraud trial to take place at the Old Bailey, the Stansted aircraft hijacking, and the attempt to extradite the fraudulent financier Roger Levitt from America to the UK.

We had dinner one evening at the Carlton Club, a High Tory establishment in Pall Mall. We met in an oak-panelled room with portraits of Margaret Thatcher and former Conservative statesmen adorning the walls. I was impressed with Desmond's personality and legal knowledge and it emerged that he also possessed a wicked sense of humour. But if his legal knowledge was encyclopaedic, he admitted that his sporting knowledge was the opposite. He told me he knew 'sweet FA' about football – a phrase he was to use to good effect in his closing speech at the trial – but that did not bother me. My own knowledge of the game was sufficient to feed him, via Stephen Berrick, with the ammunition he needed.

It is no wonder that Desmond is one of the most respected QCs in the profession. Had he not been an eminent QC then he would almost certainly have enjoyed an outstanding career as a politician.

I once saw him on a video addressing a Conservative Party conference on a drugs-related issue. He was a magnificent orator and made a speech of Churchillian quality. This was the first time I had seen him make a minor slip during a speech. At one time he addressed the conference as 'ladies and gentlemen of the jury'. But no one seemed to mind. It later reminded me of an occasion during the first trial at Winchester when he referred to a famous West London soccer club as Queens Park Rovers! A mistake, or a very clever, calculated slip of the tongue to warm up an audience, or a jury?

On the first occasion I introduced Desmond to Hans, it was in London at the old-fashioned but impressive chambers in the Inner Temple at 2 Paper Buildings, just off the Strand. It is an awe-inspiring place, steeped in tradition and history, and a far cry from the Wimbledon football pitch. Hans was most impressed and from that moment on Desmond's knowledge of football increased, as did Hans's knowledge of the law and how it worked. We never made a move thereafter without checking with Desmond. Busy as he was with his other legal work, he always made himself available, and his advice and predictions were always spot on.

From that time onwards, the paperwork began to flow, arriving at my offices in huge boxes. In all, the volume of paperwork generated by the trial totalled some 10,000 pages of evidence, accompanied by graphs, charts and documents which were methodically prepared by the CPS. Their charts, in particular, impressed me, although I never told them, of course! But I got to know the CPS and their lawyers very well. They told me that if by 10 am on any given day they had not received at least ten telephone calls relating to the case, from police, solicitors or barristers, then it was a quiet day.

When, finally, the police had compiled most of their evidence, a hearing date was set for the committal proceedings, where magistrates would have to decide whether there was a case to answer or whether to dismiss the case. I took the view that there *was* a case to answer and there was little or no possibility of the case being thrown out by a magistrates' court. Desmond de Silva felt the same. John Fashanu's lawyers held a different view as his counsel felt there was insufficient evidence. His plan was to address the magistrate on that basis and that meant there had to be a full-blown hearing, which involved calling Chris Vincent to give evidence. I therefore saw him in court for the first time. I remember my initial feeling, on seeing him in the witness box: With friends like him, who needs enemies?

Vincent admitted that he did not know Hans Segers, and when I cross-examined him in court he admitted that he had never met him, spoken to him or had had a telephone conversation with him.

Thank God for that! Our case for the defence was on track.

Bruce Grobbelaar had different problems, because he clearly knew Vincent well. I remember feeling sorry for Bruce, because someone whom Bruce had treated so well had then turned on his best friend like a viper, purely for financial reasons. It was not until the first trial at Winchester that Bruce, through his counsel, Rodney Klevan, had the opportunity of hammering Vincent in the witness box. I had never seen anybody have their personality and credibility ripped to shreds in such a way in a witness box before. Rodney did a first-class job and totally destroyed Vincent.

The magistrate would not accept the argument of John Fashanu's counsel that there was no case to answer and, as predicted by Desmond, the matter was set down for trial at Winchester Crown Court. That day at the magistrates' court was the last occasion when I defended Hans alone. As the months went by, our team developed into a close and very strong unit.

When we sat down with Desmond and Stephen for our first in-depth conference, it was clear that Desmond had read all the paperwork in advance and had a phenomenal mind for detail. He was able to cut through the irrelevant material and go straight to the heart of the problem area with the precision of a surgeon. Sometimes, when you have a conference with counsel, especially on a long case, they have not had time to read all the paperwork. But I had no doubt that Desmond had read every word. He homed in on the things Hans had foolishly admitted at the police station without me being there in his corner, and I remember him saying to Hans: 'Not very good, is it?' That was an understatement. As was widely reported, Hans had admitted to stealing expensive cars. None of this was true and we spent the next two years trying to explain this away.

Although we had had several meetings with other defence teams, my priority now was to obtain an acquittal for Hans. There was a certain amount of overlap between the cases of the various accused, but my sole concern was with Hans. The other defendants would take their advice from their own defence teams.

Accordingly, meetings usually took place between Hans and myself in my offices, followed by consultations with Desmond de Silva and Stephen Berrick. There were a few joint meetings where common ground was discussed by the various defence solicitors. Hans usually took a back seat at these and frequently kept to a middle ground, while John Fashanu and his advisers tended to direct matters.

Ultimately, each defendant took his own legal advice, which in our case was always guided by Desmond. The main thrust of our defence was that Hans was involved in match forecasting as opposed to match fixing, and that this took place in Holland and not in England. We also argued that the FA rules applied only to England and so these matters were outside their jurisdiction, but, in any event, match forecasting was not illegal. This was the crux of our defence.

Before the trial itself, there were two preliminary hearings at Winchester Crown Court and the High Court, where the gravity of the situation hit home to all concerned. These hearings were to determine what evidence was admissible, how many witnesses were to be called, and, indeed, whether there should be four separate trials, one for each defendant. We had numerous consultations with Desmond and Stephen before the hearings and looked at all the video evidence. Desmond advised me that a statement from a leading goalkeeper who was well respected would be a powerful part of our defence strategy, and I suggested the former Arsenal goalkeeper, Bob Wilson. I have been a lifelong Arsenal supporter and Bob has long been one of my favourite players. By coincidence, Grobbelaar also decided to ask Bob for his help.

The police had videos of nineteen different football matches involving Wimbledon in which Hans had played. Hans came in and sat with me in the office when we first went through them. I then spent many an evening and weekend viewing the matches at home. Much as I love the game, I did get a case of football indigestion.

I made an appointment to see Bob Wilson, whom I knew well from his Arsenal days, and he invited me to his home just before Christmas 1996. Both he and his wife Meg were charming and caring people, who gave us lots of their time. Bob is a goalkeeping coach to David Seaman at Arsenal and is now a leading sports presenter at ITV, having moved over from the BBC. For me, it was difficult not to keep talking about Arsenal, but when we got down to talking business, the first thing Bob said was that every footballer makes a number of mistakes in every match. The better players just make fewer mistakes. He discussed one particular goal that he had conceded to Steve Heighway of Liverpool, unfortunately in an FA Cup Final, when Heighway had beaten him at the near post. I remembered it well! He said usually players should not score at the near post, but would anyone say that he had made a deliberate mistake and tried to throw the game? He said that if you look at all of the goals scored every week in professional soccer, you will see a fair number of absolutely crazy goals where defenders and goalkeepers have made dreadful, schoolboy mistakes. But would you then say those mistakes were deliberate and orchestrated?

Bob Wilson struck me as such an honest man, who would never cheat in any way. He said he could never imagine any professional footballer deliberately throwing a game. He told me what a nice chap he thought Hans Segers was and how Hans had helped him out by appearing in one of Bob's goalkeeping clinics for schoolboys during the summer holidays. Hans had not wanted paying for his time. The T-shirt was enough. He always gave the youngsters plenty of time and sound advice.

After discussing the matches involving Hans which the police were investigating, Bob agreed to watch the videos and provide me with a detailed report. He also said he would be glad to give evidence on Hans's behalf at the trial. He never asked for any fee, although as an expert witness he was entitled to be paid - and I made sure he was.

Bob expertly analysed each and every goal, as he did on a weekly basis with David Seaman. I joked that Seaman did not let in many goals, so Bob did not have a lot of work to do! Bob countered by saying that because he did his job so well, Seaman also had little to do. We both laughed. I knew that if we called Bob to give evidence he would be an outstanding witness, and in the end I was proved right. In fact, he was one of the best witnesses I have ever seen.

2

THE FOOTBALL TRIAL OF THE CENTURY

Most national newspapers had teams of investigative reporters sniffing out as much background material as they could. Those reporters with good contacts in the police and Crown Prosecution Service were obviously able to keep one step ahead of their rivals and supply their newsdesk with a steady flow of so-called exclusives.

Of all the preview pieces published in the media, my favourite article appeared in *The Express* on 11 January 1997. Penned by football writer Shaun Custis, the article contained many tongue-in-cheek references to the legal formation soon to be lining up in soccer's trial of the century.

He wrote: 'The referee is Judge Justice Tuckey. Educated in Zimbabwe, but fifteen years' experience as a QC will help to remove any suspicion that referees from Africa are a little naïve. The senior judge on the Western circuit, he is not easily swayed by the big occasion.

'David Calvert-Smith will be the prosecuting counsel. He is the top man for such cases and made his name as a prosecutor in terrorist trials.

'Calvert-Smith also represented the Serious Fraud Office in the case against former Polly Peck chairman Asil Nadir. A lone man up front for the prosecution, his £500,000-a-year earnings are of a Premiership standard. He played a similar role against Asil Nadir, but failed to score when the defendant skipped bail before he could be tried on fraud and theft charges.

'Calvert-Smith will come up against a formidable four-man defence. The most flamboyant character is Desmond de Silva, QC, Hans Segers's defence counsel. He owns an island in the Indian Ocean and is married to Princess Katarina of Yugoslavia, a descendant of Queen Victoria.

'De Silva's most recent high-profile case was defending Lord Brocket, the disgraced peer jailed for five years for a £4.5 million insurance swindle involving his collection of Ferrari sports cars.

'Appearing for Bruce Grobbelaar is Rodney Klevan, QC. His CV includes successful defences of TV and radio presenter Stuart Hall and former Liverpool council leader Derek Hatton.

'Fashanu will be defended by the relatively unknown Trevor Burke. At thirty-seven, he is the youngest of the defence lawyers and considered a high-flier.

'For Lim will be Jerome Lynch, whose greatest claim to fame is acting for Geoff Knights, the boyfriend of *EastEnders* star Gillian Taylforth. Lynch defended Knights when he was accused of causing grievous bodily harm to Taylforth's chauffeur, Martin Davies. Lynch claimed prejudicial pre-trial reporting meant a fair trial was imposs-ible and the judge agreed, dismissing the case.

'While Fashanu has retired from the game, and Segers is without a club, Grobbelaar will provide an unusual sideline to the trial. As Plymouth's current first-choice keeper, he is expected to continue playing throughout the case.

'Tomorrow he will play for Zimbabwe against Togo in a World Cup qualifier and will get back just in time for the start of the trial.'

What Shaun did not know was the heartache surrounding the

selection of Bruce Grobbelaar's legal team. The original QC, Andrew Rankin, withdrew with a foot problem and one of Bruce's solicitors, Brian Canavan, developed cancer halfway through the case. He reappeared gaunt at the second trial, but died shortly thereafter. Rodney Klevan was the substitute and witty QC chosen to replace Andrew Rankin.

The defence lawyers managed to get a court order preventing the BBC from showing a drama entitled The Fix, about the 1960s soccer match-fixing case involving the Sheffield Wednesday players Peter Swan, Tony Kaye and Bronco Lane, who later moved to Everton. Minimal amounts of money were apparently involved in that particular case, masterminded by a crooked bookmaker, but all three pleaded guilty to rigging matches and were sent to prison. We successfully argued that there was a risk of prejudice of a fair trial if the film was seen by jury members. Before the trial began, John Fashanu and Bruce Grobbelaar also petitioned the High Court to have the trial adjourned until after the case had been heard against the chief prosecution witness, Chris Vincent, who had been charged with attempting to pervert the course of justice. But the judge insisted that the trial should go ahead, starting on 14 January 1997.

My assistant, Jan Cook, who had been an enormous help to me in collating all the evidence, now began the pleasant task of selecting a hotel in Winchester. We knew we would be there for two or three months. What we did not know was that there was going to be an action replay soon afterwards and that that period would turn into four or five months.

After receiving proposals from most of the best hotels in Winchester, we selected the Wykeham Arms as our battle headquarters by a narrow vote. Really this was a pub rather than a hotel, albeit a rather splendid one - which we knew would please Desmond de Silva - and the rooms were all luxurious. It proved to be a sound choice.

Jan and I travelled down on the eve of the trial with the boxes of files, which by then were so vast that we hardly had room to get into the car. I shall never forget the night we arrived at the court, at about 8pm. We had phoned in advance to make sure the court would be open, because normally it would close for business at around 4pm each day. The court staff, as ever, were extremely helpful and allowed us to use trolleys to ferry in case after case of material vital to the days ahead. It took Jan and me a couple of hours to unload the car and to build up the legal boxes, which came flatpacked like something from MFI. Jan rapidly became an expert in building the boxes and subsequently acquired the nickname 'Boxing Helena', the name of a film that had recently been released.

We took the opportunity of taking in the atmosphere of the historic Court Three, where the trial would be held. This was the same courtroom used for the Rosemary West 'House of Horror' trial a year or so earlier. On 22 November 1995, she was sentenced to ten life terms for mass murder. By coincidence, Rodney Klevan had connection with that particular case. He had been due to defend Fred West at the murder trial before West hanged himself. And the presenting counsel in the Rosemary West trial, Brian Leveson QC, later prosecuted Bruce and Hans in the FA proceedings in December 1997. It was yet another of the astonishing coincidences that seemed to crop up throughout this whole amazing episode. I was to represent Hans at that FA hearing.

Jan and I looked at the dock and envisaged the sinister Rosemary West standing there, knowing that the next day there in the dock would stand three world-famous footballers plus Mr Lim. Regulars at the Wykeham Arms told me that the Rosemary West trial was so traumatic that even the judge needed counselling.

The next day, our battle would commence. We checked in at the hotel and they gave us a warm welcome. We met up with Desmond and Stephen for supper and then settled in to our rooms. We were all under strain and the responsibility was huge. We were protecting our client's freedom and the newspapers had already written that the defendants faced up to seven years in prison if found guilty. However, spirits were high, with the jovial Desmond marshalling his troops and always appearing so positive.

We arranged to meet Hans at the hotel at 10 the following

morning. The prosecuting counsel, David Calvert-Smith, a man for whom I had a great deal of respect both professionally and as a person, was staying in the same hotel. He was a keen sportsman himself and we frequently had breakfast together. In the early days Hans and Bruce joined us for breakfast, but David Calvert-Smith felt this was not a good idea and subsequently we arranged to take our morning coffee in a different room. Sharing breakfast with someone whose job it is to put you away is hardly sensible!

Hans was a good time-keeper. He arrived punctually, as usual, with the supportive Astrid, who looked as glamorous as ever. They both tried to smile through the pressure, although there was no doubt in my mind that they were exceptionally worried. I understood their anxieties and tried not to let mine show. Everyone put on a brave face as we entered court.

But I always thought we would win.

On arrival at the court, we were greeted by hordes of photographers and press reporters, who were penned behind barriers and even hanging from trees overlooking the historic cobbled courtyard at the entrance. The old, original Winchester court was on the right, up a series of decaying steps which were being renovated. The new, modern court building was to the left.

As we climbed the steps and entered the doors, we knew we were about to embark on a case of immense proportions. Our lives would never be the same again.

3

TRIAL ONE: EARLY ATTACKS

The opening day of any trial sees the jury sworn in. Many of the proposed jury members in our trial were excused for family or health reasons, and one because he described himself as a committed Liverpool supporter. There was a moment of hilarity when the duration of the trial was discussed. The judge suggested that the case might last for eight weeks, and then said: 'But I wouldn't bet on it.'

Prosecuting counsel David Calvert-Smith went for the jugular straight from the off. His opening speech was so strong that we all went home that day with our heads down. We were to have many bad days. Fortunately, the good ones outnumbered the bad.

The charges were as follows:

REGINA VS LIM, FASHANU, SEGERS, GROBBELAAR

Heng Suan (otherwise known as Richard) Lim, John Fashanu, Hans

Johannes Cornelius Segers and Bruce David Grobbelaar are charged as follows:

Count 1

Statement of Offence: Conspiracy to give and accept corrupt payments, contrary to Section One (1) of the Criminal Law Act 1977.
Particulars of Offence: Heng Suan (Richard) Lim, John Fashanu and Hans Johannes Cornelius Segers on divers day between the 1st day of February 1991 and the 9th day of November 1994 conspired together and with others known and unknown corruptly to give and corruptly to accept gifts of money as inducements improperly to influence or attempt to influence the outcome of football matches or as rewards for having done so.

Count 2

Statement of Offence: Conspiracy to give and accept corrupt payments, contrary to Section One (1) of the Criminal Law Act 1977.
Particulars of Offence: Heng Suan (Richard) Lim, John Fashanu, and Bruce David Grobbelaar on divers day between the 1st day of November 1992 and the 9th day of November 1994 conspired together and with others known and unknown corruptly to give and corruptly to accept gifts of money as inducements improperly to influence the outcome of football matches or as rewards for having done so.

Count 3

Statement of Offence: Corruption, contrary to Section One (1) of the Prevention of Corruption Act 1996.
Particulars of Offence: Bruce David Grobbelaar on the 3rd day of November 1994 being an agent of Southampton Football Club corruptly accepted from Christopher James Edward Vincent the sum of £2,000 as an inducement or reward for doing an act in relation to the affairs of business of his principal namely for improperly influencing or attempting to influence the outcome of a football match or matches.

As you can see, Hans Segers appeared on only one charge, and Count 3 deals specifically with the sting operation mounted against Bruce Grobbelaar by *The Sun* newspaper in conjunction with Chris Vincent.

Each member of the jury was handed a large bundle of information giving details of the time of telephone conversations alleged to have taken place between the defendants, plus details of their financial positions. This was a small selection of the 10,000 documents prepared by the police and Crown Prosecution Service in connection with the trial.

David Calvert-Smith detailed his allegations as follows:

Count 1:

He alleged there was agreement between the defendants that Mr Grobbelaar would accept large sums from a Far Eastern betting syndicate for helping to achieve results in football matches in which he played as a goalkeeper, first for Liverpool and later for Southampton. He said the idea was that he would do what he could on the pitch to influence the result of games in order that the syndicate could more safely bet on the result.

The Crown alleged that Lim, a Malaysian businessman, was the representative of the syndicate in this country and made some of the early payments to Grobbelaar.

Fashanu, they said, was an associate of both Grobbelaar and Lim who was responsible for handing over the one substantial sum allegedly paid out to Grobbelaar, namely £40,000 on 21 November 1993 following the Liverpool–Newcastle match that month.

The prosecution argued that Grobbelaar had admitted on tape and on video that he was party to an agreement to accept these corrupt awards.

Mr Calvert-Smith asked: 'How can one player guarantee the result of a match? He can't. He may never have the opportunity. His fellow players, or the opposition, may frustrate him, as happened in a celebrated Liverpool–Manchester United game.

'There is a limit to what you can do in front of 50,000 people and a *Match of the Day* audience of millions. However, goalies do make genuine mistakes and therefore the odd deliberate one may escape. If you are a betting man, and wish to tip the odds in your favour, the goalkeeper is the most obvious single player to approach. If the money was corruptly given and received, it does not matter whether the result owed everything, little or nothing to the assistance of the corrupt player.'

The evidence supporting Count 1, said Mr Calvert-Smith, came from four principal sources: evidence from Chris Vincent, telephone evidence, documentary evidence, and lies told by Bruce Grobbelaar when confronted with the allegation by reporters from *The Sun*.

Mr Calvert-Smith said that Vincent squandered all the money given to him by Grobbelaar to invest in a safari park business and then approached *The Sun* to set up a 'sting' operation.

Mr Calvert-Smith admitted that Vincent 'is a witness for whom most if not all will have little sympathy.' He added: 'His decision to expose Grobbelaar's activities was the result of a business quarrel and not a desire to prevent corruption. The decision to expose Grobbelaar through *The Sun* was a desire to enrich himself. He had already been paid substantial sums for his story by various media outlets and was in negotiation with a publisher to produce a book.

'There is therefore every reason to scrutinize his evidence with great care before accepting it as true. He has recently been charged with a serious offence in which it is alleged that he asked Fashanu for a large sum of money to disappear and not give evidence at this trial. He has not been tried and will not be tried by you, but the Crown invite you at this stage, in fairness to these defendants, to assume his guilt of that charge. If the matter is investigated by counsel in cross-examination or otherwise at this trial, then it will be a matter for you to decide what conclusion you come to and whether that conclusion helps you to decide innocence or guilt.'

Count 2:

Mr Calvert-Smith said that a similar agreement existed between the defendants so that Hans Segers would accept large sums of money

(*top*) Hans (front row, third from left) in his school football team in 1972.

(*below*) Hans (front row, third from left) with the team at PSV Eindhoven in the 1982-83 season.

(left) Hans and Astrid, (below) Hans and Astrid with Nicky and Brigitte.

(opposite) Hans takes a break in training with Vinnie Jones while at Wimbledon (Express Newspapers).

(left) Astrid leaving the family home in Fleet on the day the news about Hans broke; (below) Hans leaving Eastleigh police station after being questioned by police.

Mel Goldberg in his office. *(Tim Anderson)*

Hans Segers' legal team makes their way to Winchester Crown Court. From left to right: Mel Goldberg, Astrid Segers, Hans Segers, Desmond de Silva and Stephen Berrick.

Celebrations after the verdict.

Hans celebrates a heroic performance at the end of Wolves' FA Cup
Quarter Final clash with Leeds. (Action Images)

from a Far Eastern betting syndicate for helping to achieve results in Wimbledon matches. The idea was the same, he said, that he would do what he could on the pitch to influence the result of games in order that the syndicate could more safely bet on their outcome.

The Crown claimed that Fashanu was an associate of Segers (he played for the same team) and Lim. There were distinct signs, said Mr Calvert-Smith, that Lim's role was being taken over by Fashanu.

Segers paid large sums of cash into a Swiss branch of an American bank during the football season 1993–4. They were not his wages or from any other legal source, he said. Mr Calvert-Smith added: 'He was to claim in interview that the money was the proceeds of crimes committed by him in the 1970s and that the cash had been drawn on an account in Jersey. The Crown has been unable to find any evidence of this account and Mr Segers has kept the identity of any such account to himself.'

Mr Calvert-Smith then claimed that large sums of money came into England from the Far East and that Segers and Fashanu made large payments into the same bank. He claimed there was telephone and documentary evidence to confirm contact between the defendants, but he admitted that there was no evidence of any kind to suggest any contact between Grobbelaar and Segers.

Count 3:

This concerned the *Sun* 'sting' operation in which the newspaper gave Vincent £2,000 to see whether Grobbelaar would accept it.

Mr Calvert-Smith said: 'As you will see and hear from the tapes, videos and transcripts, Vincent tried to and succeeded in interesting Grobbelaar in working for a second, totally fictitious syndicate. The £2,000 was to be the first of a regular series of advance payments until the big match later in the season when, if things went according to plan, he would get £100,000.'

Mr Calvert-Smith described the Crown's version of events to the jury. He said: 'On 8 November 1994, Grobbelaar went to Gatwick airport to catch a plane to Zimbabwe. He was going to play for his country. At about 4.30pm, he was challenged by reporters from

The Sun newspaper, with allegations that he had been part of the corrupt schemes, now Counts 1 and 3. After speaking to them and by telephone to the editor of *The Sun*, he changed his plans and must have flown home to Liverpool. Next day the story broke in *The Sun* and parts of the video interview were played on TV. There appeared to be serious criminal offences alleged and so the police in Hampshire became involved. The first targets of investigation were obvious – *The Sun* recordings and the two participants, Vincent and Grobbelaar.

'Vincent was briefly interviewed and a statement was taken from him on 16 November. Grobbelaar, by then living in Southampton, was visited on the day of his return from Zimbabwe, on 17 November 1994. He was seen at Southampton's training ground and asked to come with the police, bringing his personal property. They went to his home, which was searched. A couple of the documents from that search are in your bundle,' Mr Calvert-Smith told the jury. He was interviewed under caution. His solicitor advised him not to answer any questions and he followed that advice.

'Enquiries then proceeded into the case and Vincent gave a detailed statement. Grobbelaar's telephone bills were carefully scrutinized and began to reveal the true picture.'

The research into telephone calls, allegedly linking Grobbelaar, Lim, Fashanu and Segers, was the main thrust of the prosecution's case, together with the evidence of Chris Vincent.

Mr Calvert-Smith described the background details of how Vincent and Grobbelaar first met. He went on: 'Vincent first came to the UK in 1989. In 1991 he registered a company in the UK called Savannah Management Ltd whose purpose was to seek out and develop UK interests in Zimbabwe, in particular safari holidays.

'In July 1992 a business acquaintance of his suggested he contact Grobbelaar to discuss a possible investment in Savannah's possible purchase of some land out there. The two men met and in due course Grobbelaar agreed to invest £20,000, and later a further £20,000. In all, he invested some £55,000. Savannah became

Mondoro Wildlife Corporation Ltd. Mondoro is Shona for "lion god", it being felt that a strong African name was appropriate.

'The two men became close friends and spent much time seeing each other and often telephoning each other. In August 1993, Grobbelaar mentioned Fashanu's name in connection with an approach he said he'd had from people in the Far East who wanted advice on the likely results of Premier League games, so that they would be able to bet on the results with the benefit of specialist knowledge. Nothing criminal in that.

'In fact, Grobbelaar, Fashanu and Lim had known each other for some time before August 1993. Enquiries into their telephone bills eventually showed that they had been in contact at least since November 1992, and Fashanu and Lim since 1991.'

David Calvert-Smith admitted there were limitations on the prosecution's evidence.

- They could not prove who made any individual call.
- They could not prove who received any individual call.
- Calls frequently lasted only a few seconds.
- There was no record of what they said to each other.
- The Crown had no access to any calls made from Indonesia to the UK.
- The Crown had incomplete telephone records – some had been lost.
- Some events could not be timed exactly.

The Crown suggested that the timing, sequence and length of the calls, together with the lack of any explanation for their phones being in contact on such a regular basis, does prove:

- The callers were the defendants or their co-conspirators.
- The calls were linked.
- And they must have been discussing the matters with which the jury was concerned.

A number of charts were produced itemizing various calls allegedly made between the defendants and Lim's Indonesian contacts, who were found to have stayed at the Dorchester Hotel in London and made calls to various parties from there.

Much of the prosecution evidence focused on Vincent's claims about his relationship with Grobbelaar and how he spent large amounts of his friend's cash.

In August 1994 the plans for the Mondoro venture fell through and Grobbelaar lost a considerable sum of money, as did the other investors involved, although not Vincent. He admitted that he had invested no money of his own in the project.

In that same month, Grobbelaar transferred to Southampton, and the prosecution alleged that calls between him and Lim then resumed after a quiet spell when Grobbelaar had been dropped from the Liverpool first team.

By now Fashanu had also changed clubs, moving from Wimbledon to Aston Villa.

It was on 6 September that Vincent went to *The Sun* with his story. After discussions between him and the newspaper, it was agreed that he would attempt to interest Grobbelaar in a new, fictitious syndicate. The *Sun* hoped that if Grobbelaar showed an interest in joining this new syndicate, it would show that what Vincent had said about the old syndicate was true.

Police enquiries led to Grobbelaar, Fashanu, Lim and Segers being arrested on 14 March 1995 and their homes and offices were searched. Diaries and documents were seized and used as evidence. When arrested, Lim and Fashanu declined to answer questions.

But Hans Segers did answer. And, said Mr Calvert-Smith, he told officers of his various bank accounts. He said he had a Swiss bank account opened three years earlier. Hans said much of this money was his savings from his earnings in Holland and from activities outside football, such as Ties International. He also admitted being a car thief, but had never been prosecuted or arrested for this. He told police that as a youngster, he had once been taken to a police station for stealing a bottle of Coke. He also admitted that his father had once found some stolen property in his room and had taken him to the police station. He said he moved money from his Jersey account to his Swiss bank to avoid paying tax.

The prosecution alleged that money was paid from Indonesia

into Lim's account and Lim would then pay John Fashanu's wife. The Crown stated that Fashanu and Segers would often pay sums of money into the same bank days after Wimbledon had lost matches. They said that telephone contact between the defendants stopped after *The Sun* had published allegations about Grobbelaar.

The above allegations were, of course, denied by Hans.

4

HANS IN THE WITNESS BOX

When Hans went into the witness box, he was asked by Desmond de Silva: 'Have you ever thrown a game of football in your life?'

Hans replied: 'Never. I have never thrown a match. I have never been asked to throw a match. I am a winner.'

Hans described his career as it developed with PSV Eindhoven and led to a transfer to England, first to Nottingham Forest and then on to Wimbledon. 'Moving to England to play in the Premiership was like a dream come true,' he said. Hans told the court that in 1994 he was earning £1,000 a week with Wimbledon, plus a signing-on fee of £30,000 and a loyalty bonus of £50,000. He also received a £500 bonus every time he kept a clean sheet.

I remember referring to my notes and looking at the entries for Wednesday 12 February 1997, Day 20 of the first trial. It was a tough day for Hans. He did well answering questions from Desmond but not so well in cross-examination by David Calvert-Smith, who was clearly sharpening his cutting edge on Hans. My note said: 'Is he warming up for Bruce?'

I noticed David Calvert-Smith looking up to the gallery after his cross-examination of Hans. He knew he had done well. Desmond stood up and Hans looked at him like a lost mountaineer seeing a St Bernard rescue dog delivering brandy!

All the defendants appeared fairly upbeat during the trial and I thought Hans stood up well to the enormous psychological pressure. They all put on a brave face and all seemed confident that they would win. Naturally, there were highs and lows. But as I mentioned before, the good days outnumbered the bad. Hans always got on well with the other defendants, although before the trial he hardly knew Bruce apart from in his professional capacity. There was always a good sense of humour among them.

Desmond gave clear instructions at all times as to how he intended to conduct the defence. He grilled Hans for hours, running through the evidence. Although much of it did not relate personally to Hans, it was still necessary to read it all to make sure and it took months to go through all 10–15,000 pages with a fine-tooth comb.

Because of the sensational nature of the case, all the national newspapers devoted a huge amount of space to the allegations being made in court, which they were free to report. At one stage during the trial, *The Sun* published a two-page spread detailing results of Wimbledon matches alleged to have been fixed. However, Hans pointed out that the 1993–4 season in question was one of the most successful in the club's history. 'We finished in the top six and that equalled the best position Wimbledon have ever achieved,' he said.

Desmond asked: 'Was it successful because you were throwing matches?'

'No, I don't think so,' was Hans's reply.

Desmond then asked Hans if he had ever received money or indeed the offer of money for throwing a game. Hans replied: 'No. Never. Nobody ever asked me to throw a game and I never have thrown a game.'

Hans was asked about his sources of income outside football. He explained how he was a partner in a ties business that was active throughout Europe, and that he was doing some commentating for Dutch TV, and providing forecasts on Dutch matches for Richard Lim. He said he paid in some of the money to a Dutch bank account and some of it was paid to him in cash when his business partner travelled to England from Holland. He paid that money into the London branch of a Swiss bank for tax reasons.

Hans was asked if Wimbledon players bet on the outcome of matches. He said that quite a few bet on the name of the scorer of the first goal in a match, but he was not aware of any players gambling on results, and certainly not on their own games.

He said he had first spoken to Richard Lim in 1992 when John Fashanu had asked his advice about cars: 'John knew I was involved in cars and I bought and sold them quite frequently. Richard wanted my help in selling his car.' Hans remembered the first time he met Lim in Fashanu's offices in London: 'He had a proposal for me. He had some friends who were betting on English games but they wanted to start betting on Dutch games and so, with me being a Dutchman and quite knowledgeable about Dutch football, he asked if I could give him some information and say what the results would be. Although I had left Holland, I still kept in touch with Dutch football on satellite TV, football magazines and Teletext.'

Hans explained that he agreed to a fee of £1,000 a week to forecast Dutch matches, but Fashanu had negotiated the fee up to £1,500 a week. He told the court that he would forecast Dutch matches but would also provide Lim with information on English teams, usually the opponents Wimbledon had played the previous week. He did not supply forecasts on English results because Lim was an expert himself. Hans said he did not think he was breaking any law supplying forecasts of Dutch matches or his thoughts on English football. When Desmond asked him if he knew this might be against FA rules, Hans replied: 'At the time, no.'

Once he had been alerted by a *Daily Mirror* reporter to a possible match-fixing scandal breaking, Hans had become deeply concerned. He then read the FA rules relating to gambling and was worried about any possible action. He spoke to other players and to the the Wimbledon owner Sam Hammam, and realized he could be facing a problem for his role in forecasting the results of matches.

When asked by Desmond if he had told the truth to the police at first, Hans replied: 'No, I did not.'

Desmond asked: 'How would you describe most of your answers?'

Hans: 'Absolute rubbish.' He had told the police he did not know Lim and had never spoken to him.

Hans explained: 'If I had admitted to knowing Mr Lim, the police were going to ask me about all the telephone calls and I would have had to say that I was doing forecasting for Richard.' Asked what the consequences of that might have been, Hans replied that the former Swindon Town manager Lou Macari had been in trouble for betting against his own team and that the club had been relegated by the FA after having in fact gained promotion. 'With that in mind, there was no way I was going to admit to knowing Richard or say I was doing the forecasting,' he said.

Desmond: 'Because your forecasting was going to lead to betting?'

Hans: 'Yes. That's correct.'

When Hans was asked about his account of stealing cars in Holland, Desmond said: 'You're smiling.'

Hans replied: 'Yes, I am smiling because it was absolute rubbish. When they first took me into custody, first of all I had to explain where I got the money from, and I did not want to admit that I was doing forecasting. Had I admitted the money had come from Ties International, I would have had the taxman on my back. I thought if I just made up a story that the money is coming from activities in Holland, then I won't have any problems with the taxman and no problems with the FA.'

He added: 'I couldn't bear the thought of getting banned here in England. That's something I just couldn't think about.'

Hans also admitted that he lied to police about his relationship with John Fashanu. He explained that he and Fashanu were both involved in affairs and would often cover for each other. 'Astrid had showed me the yellow card,' said Hans. 'When the arrest was made, my marriage was back together and I thought if anything pops out, I will risk losing my wife, losing my kids, everything.'

Fashanu was alleged to be seeing a famous female singer, and Desmond asked: 'Were you prepared to let down your friend and name names?'

Hans said: 'No way.'

Desmond asked Hans why he told the police that the money in the Swiss bank had come from a Jersey account. 'It's the same thing as before,' said Hans. 'If I mentioned another bank abroad, then I would not have to pay tax on it.'

In fact, the Inland Revenue were taking a deep interest in all of the defendants and the sums of money alleged to have been involved. Hans added: 'When I arrived at the court I saw two chairs, one for the FA and one for the taxman.' Smiling and pointing to a figure at the back of the court, he added: 'The gentleman over there with the big smile, I think that's Mr Taxman.'

Hans was obviously fairly relaxed by now, answering questions fluently, although at the start of the case he found the proceedings quite nerve-racking. He said he had received between £45,000 and £48,000 in the years from 1993 to 1995. The prosecution had said that there was a pattern of telephone calls before matches were lost, but Hans said it was the same whether it was a win, loss or a draw. He said it was 'absolute rubbish' to suggest the pattern related only to losing matches.

When asked how he gave information to Lim, Hans said he would meet up in Fashanu's office in London, usually after training on a Thursday afternoon. He would discuss details of matches and pass on his knowledge of Dutch football. If he learned of any extra information, such as an injury to a key player, he would telephone Lim to pass on the news. Lim would also contact him to check details before he passed on information to Indonesia.

The two players kept in touch after Fashanu's move to Aston Villa because they were involved in a property transaction in London. They had decided to purchase a repossessed flat in St John's Wood, have the property decorated and then rent it out.

Hans told the court he had received approximately £75,000 from Fashanu towards the property venture.

When asked about his time with Wimbledon FC, Hans said: 'Joe Kinnear was a great manager. He was honest, he was straight and he knew his stuff.' He told the court that all of Wimbledon's matches were videoed and that Joe Kinnear would spend a considerable time analysing the games and looking for any faults. Asked if he had been criticized by the manager, Hans replied: 'When you play at Wimbledon, you don't escape any criticism.' He said that if his manager had suspected he was guilty of deliberately throwing games then he would never have been picked again, let alone go on to play three hundred games for the club.

Hans said he did not know that Lim was also using Grobbelaar for assistance in forecasting matches. He described Bruce as 'a great goalkeeper and a great man', but did not know him on a personal level. They had played against each other many times, at opposite ends of the field, and he had met him once at a charity golf day.

The case then developed into an extension of *Match of the Day* as the curtains were drawn in the courtroom and the jury were shown video highlights of a number of goals being scored against Wimbledon. The jury, the barristers and defendants were given headphones to listen to the commentaries, each of about four minutes, as the extracts were shown on three screens inside the court, one for the jury, one for the judge, and one for the lawyers. The public and the press were able to watch the action unfold on the lawyers' screen, situated high up behind the clerk of the court.

Hans said he had no chance of stopping any of the goals scored against him. When asked what would happen if the goalkeeper was always in the right place, he answered: 'Then nobody would ever score.' He said the ball would often travel at speeds of up to 90 miles per hour and, as modern footballs were quite light, the path of a shot would often dip or deviate while the ball was in the air.

Desmond de Silva told the court that Wimbledon had suffered a disastrous sequence of results in the 1995–6 season, failing to win any of fourteen matches while Hans was out of the side recovering from a knee operation. When Hans returned to the side in late December, they started winning again.

One match which had attracted particular attention was Wimbledon's 3–2 defeat away at Everton on the final day of the 1993–4 season. Wimbledon had been leading 2–0 earlier in the match but the result saved Everton from relegation. The video of Everton's third goal was studied in some detail. Bob Wilson, called as a witness for the defence, pointed out that the ball had changed direction after a bad bounce on a well-worn pitch. He gave the judge a lesson in 'narrowing the angle' – a phrase which the judge at the second trial did not fully appreciate – and told the jury about the skills required as a goalkeeper. He explained that one of the most important elements of a goalkeeper's art is the 'barrier' save, an expression I had not heard before. This means standing up tall when facing a striker, using every part of your body to make as big a barrier as possible to stop his shot from reaching the net.

While preparing his evidence, Bob had painstakingly made notes on each match, running and rewinding the video recorder to isolate incidents that he felt were relevant to his analysis. Nowhere, in the many hours of videotape evidence, could he find a single incident that looked remotely questionable.

I will never forget the day Bob was called as a witness at Winchester. He faced a fierce attack from the prosecuting counsel, but maintained his poise, authority and dignity to deliver evidence in such a thorough and professional way that the jury should have been left in no doubt that Hans was innocent. The prosecution referred to a 'goalkeepers' club', but Bob reminded them that when a goalkeeper was 'out of line', such as the West German Harald Schumacher in a World Cup match some years ago against France when he rushed out of his area to flatten a French forward, he would be the first to criticize him. He gave that impressive answer to a prosecution question, so he could not have known it was coming and it was not a 'rehearsed' answer. Well done, Bob. What a man to have on your side.

Very few people knew that Bob Wilson was concealing a very distressing family matter. His daughter was seriously ill. Yet still he insisted on turning up at the court and delivering his evidence in the calm, unflappable manner that has been the hallmark of his years in television.

5

DON'T MENTION THE TWO GRAND!

By the end of the trial everybody knew how to keep goal, even if some of us were not big enough or young enough to put into practice what we had learnt about the arts of goalkeeping. Rodney Klevan, in his closing speech, joked that Desmond de Silva would have made an outstanding goalkeeper, referring more to his bulk than his speed off the mark, unless, of course, he was heading for the bar!

Remarks like these flew thick and fast as the courtroom at times resembled a combination of *Match of the Day*, *Ironside* and *They Think It's All Over*. Although no one lost sight of the fact that the players' freedom was on the line and that football itself was on trial, *Regina v Grobbelaar, Fashanu, Segers and Lim* offered the normally staid wearers of wigs and gowns the opportunity to indulge in verbal exchanges that had more in common with foot-ball's culture of dressing-room banter than serious, stodgy, dull legal arguments.

In the first trial, Mr Justice Tuckey, a most respected judge with a sense of humour, allowed both prosecution and defence lawyers a certain amount of leeway and latitude in addressing the court. He was a commercial judge as opposed to a criminal judge, and quite different from the stern Mr Justice McCullough in the second trial. Quips about favourite football teams abounded, and there were several amusing episodes when famous footballing personalities appeared in the witness box.

The Aston Villa goalkeeper Mark Bosnich forgot to address his answers to counsel or the judge and began to pontificate like Rumpole of the Bailey. At one stage, he prefixed an answer with the words, 'Ladies and gentlemen of the jury, I beg you to consider . . .' before being reminded of the practices of a court of law. (When John Fashanu transferred from Wimbledon to Aston Villa, he lodged for several months with Bosnich. With two other goalkeepers already under suspicion, the police interviewed Bosnich in connection with the case.)

Before going into court, the defendants had regular meetings with their solicitors to discuss the way in which the case was unfolding. The combination of professional footballers' banter and the dry, understated wit of their bewigged representatives produced some fascinating verbal encounters. When it was learned that a juror was to be dismissed during the first trial, the players were having friendly bets as to the identity of the person involved! In the jury box, the seats were arranged in three rows of four. So when the juror was discharged, Bruce Grobbelaar quipped, 'Now they'll be in 4-4-3 formation.' It was rumoured that the juror had been apprehended leaving a public house after recounting stories about the case to his mates. The police had been tipped off by an anonymous caller.

The former Norwich City player Jeremy Goss gave the shortest evidence I have ever seen in court. He flew all the way down from Edinburgh, where he was now playing for Hearts, to tell the court his name and address and the fact that he was very disappointed that Bruce Grobbelaar had saved one of his shots when Norwich played Liverpool in a particular match at Carrow Road. 'I expected to score and Bruce made a blinding save,' said Goss. That was the end of his evidence and he left. The purpose of his visit, however, was to underline the defence claim that Bruce was trying his best to stop shots reaching the back of the net in a match the prosecution suggested he was trying to rig.

Ron Atkinson, a manager renowned for delivering witty one-liners at his after-match press conferences, did not disappoint the gallery.

Ron was then director of football at Coventry City. 'One day I was looking for my colleagues in the lunch break and said: "I cannot find my defence team anywhere." '

Ron replied: 'Neither could I at Coventry for three years.'

When Rodney Klevan was questioning Atkinson, he asked: 'Is it true that some teams always win and other teams always lose?'

Atkinson replied: 'I suppose so.'

Klevan: 'Then why does my team always lose?'

Atkinson: 'Probably because you support Brighton and Hove Albion.'

Klevan then admitted that he actually supported Manchester City, and at one stage said to the judge: 'If your Lordship allows me to digress, what, Mr Atkinson, did you think of Frank Swift and Bert Trautmann?' Both were former Manchester City goalkeepers and nothing to do with the case!

Ron spoke up on behalf of Fashanu and the two goalkeepers. He said that while he was manager of Aston Villa in 1994, Fashanu had telephoned him to ask if he was interested in signing the Nigerian striker Daniel Amokachi, who later joined Everton. Atkinson said: 'I told him that I would be more interested in signing *him* (Fashanu) if he felt it was possible to get away from Wimbledon.' He said that Fashanu had always been regarded as a nuisance whenever he had played against Villa and that his players had a very healthy respect for him. 'I thought his brand of aggressiveness and competitiveness might just give us that little bit extra that we needed to maybe make us the best,' he explained.

Fashanu negotiated the move himself, but a knee injury ended his career a few months later. Atkinson said that Fashanu's presence in attack had given his Villa side a physical dimension they had not had before. He described Fashanu as very confident, a hard worker and totally honest. He more than made up for a limited ability with plenty of fire and aggression. He was not surprised that Fashanu had moved into the media field once his playing days were over.

When Atkinson was questioned by Desmond de Silva about a sequence of nine results in 1994 which produced eight defeats and one draw, Atkinson said that even the best of teams could have an appalling run.

Asked if goalkeepers were 'a breed apart', he replied: 'That's how the legend goes. They are all supposed to be crackers.'

Desmond asked him if he felt Hans was tenacious. Ron said: 'Yes. He may have been a foreign player, but he was part and parcel of what we know in football as the Wimbledon thing.' He also told the court how, when he was manager of West Bromwich Albion, he had tried to sign Bruce Grobbelaar from Durban City in 1978 but was unable to obtain a work permit, though Bruce did play in one friendly game for the Baggies.

Atkinson described Grobbelaar as an 'Indian rubber man'. He said: 'He was so agile and so zany. He told us stories of what he had done in the Rhodesian army, and that sort of thing made him stand out from other young players. Basically, he showed us that he had the ability to become a top goalkeeper.

'He was error-prone when he was a kid, and to be fair he carried that on at times through his career. But you only have to look at his career with Liverpool – and Liverpool don't sign mugs. He was part of one of the best teams Britain has ever produced. He also replaced Ray Clemence, who was one of the best goalkeepers this country has produced.'

Atkinson said that the word 'great' was over-used and that he would put three post-war English goalkeepers into that category: Gordon Banks, Peter Shilton and Clemence. Behind that, he said, was another stratum of ten or twenty very good goalkeepers, and Bruce would be one of them.

Ron was also asked by David Calvert-Smith about Fashanu's enforced retirement through injury. 'By that time I had left. That appalling run of results meant I was out of a job,' he replied. When Atkinson left the witness box, he winked at the defendants in the dock. Big man, big personality, and the star of the trial so far.

There were other amusing moments. At one time we employed a Dutch interpreter whose English was so bad it was easier to understand him when he was speaking Dutch. He was the first interpreter I have ever seen who was substituted in the middle of a game.

Then at dinner on one occasion, I was talking to Desmond de Silva in the presence of Bruce Grobbelaar's solicitor, David Hewitt. Desmond passed a comment that he hoped that Fash, with his immaculate appearance and superior manner, would not appear too grand. At which point David Hewitt quickly replied: 'Two grand? Don't mention the two grand!' That particular sum, of course, was allegedly the contents of the envelope shown on video being handed by Chris Vincent to Bruce Grobbelaar in a Southampton hotel room.

Fashanu in the end declined to give evidence in either trial. But several defence witnesses described him as a hero on and off the field. Fash, as well as being a powerful striker, was a presenter of the popular *Gladiators* TV show and was a figure of immense status in Africa, the court was told. No one knew he was not going to give evidence until 5 February 1997. He told Hans before going into court: 'Silence is an individual's right.'

Robert Smith, the executive director of the United Kingdom Committee for UNICEF, the worldwide children's charity, said that Fashanu was a special ambassador for the children of Africa. He said: 'He has an astonishing reputation in Africa, on a sporting and political level, and is immensely popular with ordinary people. He helped to rebuild the Zambian football team after the tragic accident in which the whole team were killed in an air crash. That made him a national hero in Zambia.' Mr Smith said that Fashanu had helped to promote the awareness of Aids among young people. He had also interrupted a trip to Uganda on behalf of the organization to visit neighbouring Rwanda at a time of crisis there. According to Mr Smith, Fashanu enjoyed an extraordinary status in Africa and had connections with many political leaders throughout the continent.

One of the matches under scrutiny was the famous 3-3 draw between Liverpool and Manchester United at Anfield. United had taken a 3-0 lead but Liverpool produced an astonishing fightback to secure a draw. The prosecution had planned to show highlights only, but Rodney Klevan insisted on showing the court the full ninety minutes to show the effort put in by Bruce Grobbelaar and the number of quality saves he had made. Richard Lim's junior counsel, a witty Irishman named Lewis Power, said to me: 'Mel, can you believe this? I would pay to watch this match and here we are all being paid to be here. It's like watching *Match of the Day*. Can you pass me a can of beer?'

When the compilation of the Wimbledon matches was first shown, my heart was in my mouth because I had compiled the sequence myself. I was worried the video might not work or might show the wrong matches. In fact, everything was fine. I had put in many hours of work obtaining the tapes and editing them together, although I have to admit that when I first began work on the project at home I had to ask my daughter, Nova, how to work the video recorder.

During the Liverpool-Man United match, Sky TV presenter Andy Gray remarked significantly during his commentary: 'We have had six goals and neither goalkeeper has made a mistake.' Little did he know that a Crown Court judge would be watching that tape two years later. After the video had been played, Rodney Klevan asked the judge for his permission to sit down. 'May I move from the terraces to the directors' box?' he asked amidst much laughter.

Rodney certainly enjoyed questioning the celebrity witnesses. He said to Bob Wilson: 'You are the same age as me, although you appear to be wearing better.' And he said to former Liverpool captain and *Match of the Day* analyst Alan Hansen: 'Please don't talk to me the way you talk to Jimmy Hill.'

He also asked Alan: 'Are you not free to play for Manchester City?'

Reply: 'They need a lot more than me.'

Judge: 'Whatever you do, it is clear it does not get any better.'

Rodney Klevan: 'Do you mean me or Manchester City?'

The appearance of Alan Hansen in court came as a real surprise. Normally we knew who was coming along to give evidence, but Hansen's arrival was kept secret. David Hewitt kept it well under wraps. Hansen delivered a stirring testimonial to the talents and strengths of his team-mate Bruce Grobbelaar, as did another former Liverpool man, Nigel Clough. Nigel was quietly spoken, unlike his father, and said Bruce was a good team member and the sort of goalkeeper you were proud to have in your defence.

When Rodney Klevan spoke to Gordon Banks, he said: 'You are a legend. When you made that famous save from Pele, for England in the 1970 World Cup match against Brazil, why didn't you catch the ball?' There was so much laughter that Gordon forgot to answer the question.

During the judge's summing-up in the first trial, he said: 'We all know which team Mr Klevan supports, poor man. His team should not figure high in your deliberations.' And during Desmond's closing speech in the first trial, he jokingly told the jury: 'Mr Klevan supports Manchester City. That is because his doctor has told him not to do anything too exciting.' Desmond added: 'Some people go to Buckingham Palace to watch the Changing of the Guard. Others go to Manchester City to watch the changing of the managers.'

As I mentioned in an earlier chapter, Desmond once referred to QPR as Queens Park Rovers. He also described the Wimbledon manager Joe Kinnear as Roy Kinnear, the comedian who tragically fell off his horse in Spain and died. When Desmond realized his mistake, he turned to his junior barrister Stephen Berrick and said in a loud, theatrical voice: 'Next time you pass me a note, please write more clearly.'

Something of the Crazy Gang spirit seemed to be in evidence behind the scenes. There were practical jokes galore. One of the lawyers, Andrew Eadis, had his wig removed by an unknown party from the counsels' changing-room. He had to watch proceedings from the press box because he was improperly dressed. This was the second wig to go missing during that particular week. All bald people in the court were immediately under suspicion.

Bruce Grobbelaar was frequently photographed wearing a different hat each day as he approached the court. Jerome Lynch, counsel for Richard Lim, bore a remarkable likeness to Bruce and one day decided to wear a similar hat to court. He was stopped by two young children and asked for his autograph. One day, Bruce's white Mercedes blocked Desmond's car in the hotel car park for nearly two hours. Someone suggested Bruce deserved a parking ticket, but Desmond thought a yellow card might be more appropriate. On 27 January, Bruce returned to court from Zimbabwe looking fresh and colourful in a wine-coloured blazer with a smart white raincoat. He said he had had to change planes in Frankfurt at four o'clock that morning while flying home following his side's 0-0 draw with Ghana. It may have been a goalless draw, but there was plenty of incident. As the players left the field they were forced to lie on the floor to escape attack from a swarm of bees. In another international match that punctuated the trial, Bruce had to protect the referee from a horde of angry fans who had invaded the pitch.

One week after Bruce's brush with the bees, Arsenal, my favourite team, lost 1-0 to Leeds in the FA Cup. Simon Jeal, a solicitor with the CPS, was also an Arsenal fan, so we were swapping hard-luck stories before the day's business began in court. In the second trial one of the police detectives asked me why I no longer wore my Arsenal tie to court. I replied that I was worried in case any members of the jury were Spurs supporters.

It was strange going back to one's hotel room after the day's proceedings, turning on the TV and frequently seeing yourself walking to and from court. This happened so often that it became disappointing when you turned on the TV and found that you were not in shot. When that happened, we would often give the TV reporters some gentle 'stick' the next day. On a couple of occasions, when I had to drive somewhere for a meeting after court to see a witness, I would turn on the radio to hear them describing the day's business. There was no escape.

When the court was not sitting, I used to spend much of the break time telephoning the office to pick up any messages that had been left with my secretary. I found a favourite place on the first floor, next to a window, where the reception was best for my mobile phone. Unfortunately, everyone else gradually discovered the same spot and Bruce Grobbelaar and I frequently used to vie for what I called my 'office space'. Despite the gravity of the proceedings, Bruce, like the other players, was always ready for a laugh and a joke.

I also had many chats with the taxing officer of the court, Alan Roberts, who turned out to be a Stoke City supporter. He dealt with costs and made sure we got paid! He frequently moaned about Arsenal beating Stoke in two FA Cup semi-finals in the 1970s, both of which I was present at.

After each day's hearing, the Wykeham Arms was a popular choice for many of the legal fraternity, who would meet in the early evenings for a relaxed meal and a few drinks to discuss the day's business and plan strategy for the campaign ahead. Often some of the star witnesses would also gather at the Wykeham and this tiny corner hostelry, which opened up, Tardis-like, to reveal further rooms inside, resembled a footballing Hall of Fame.

Alan Ball, one of England's 1966 World Cup-winning heroes and a former Arsenal player, joined us for a few drinks at the Wykeham one evening after giving evidence on behalf of Bruce Grobbelaar. He admitted he had been under pressure from the Southampton board and supporters to drop Bruce after the allegations had first been aired in *The Sun*, but had no hesitation in standing by him. He said Bruce was someone you could always rely on, brilliant in training and always helping the younger players. After *The Sun*'s revelations had been published, Southampton's first match was against Arsenal, and we both recalled how the Gunners fans behind Bruce's goal had taunted him by waving £5 notes in the air. Later that same evening, I had dinner with Alan, David Hewitt and his colleague David Crank at a Chinese restaurant in Winchester. Alan was full of hilarious anecdotes about football and regaled us with his stories throughout the evening. He was an Everton man through and through, and although he was a huge success with Arsenal, his heart was really still at Goodison Park. But he told us that the club where the supporters treated him the best was at Exeter City, which I found amazing considering the number of bigger clubs he has been attached to at one time or another during his long and distinguished career as a player and a manager. Another regular visitor to the Wykeham Arms was the former Liverpool player Sammy Lee. He frequently stayed there on holiday and although he was not involved with the trial in any way, I enjoyed having a drink with him. First, because he's a real character, and second, he's smaller than me!

When I returned to Winchester after the trial for a meeting with the court taxing officer, I popped into the Wykeham and was treated like a long-lost relative. We were to become, in Hans's words, part of the furniture there and I know when the trial finished we were sorely missed.

As I have mentioned, despite the laughter and the levity, at no time did we lose sight of the fact that this was a serious business. After a trial lasting eight weeks, the jury were out for eleven hours but failed to reach a verdict on any of the charges. The jury foreman sent a note to the judge explaining their predicament, and was asked if there was any reasonable prospect of arriving at a verdict. 'We do not believe so,' he told the judge.

'I think that's it,' said Mr Justice Tuckey, who then discharged the jury of eight men and three women. It was estimated that the investigation had cost the taxpayer a cool £10 million.

Prosecutor David Calvert-Smith immediately demanded a retrial. 'That is the normal procedure,' he said. 'That is the intention of the Crown and I will be taking instructions at the highest level.' Mr Justice Tuckey later told the barristers involved in the case that any retrial would have a new judge. He said: 'I will not be making any football jokes, but there will definitely be a substitute.' Bail for the defendants was extended, and plans were soon put into action for the retrial at Winchester Crown Court in the summer.

I made a statement to the media in the rain, under an umbrella held by Jan, saying how disappointed we were at having to go through the whole process again. I was quoted in the *Daily Telegraph* as saying: 'It is very unsatisfactory for the defendants, the Crown and the lawyers concerned, but I am still confident that Mr Segers will be cleared, and so is he.' Someone described my TV appearance as 'Whingeing in the rain.'

The following day's newspaper headlines were full of footballing puns. 'Trial goes to a replay,' said one. 'Let's settle it on penalties,' said another.

Despite a feeling of relief at the absence of a guilty verdict, there was a terrible sense of anticlimax. The job was only halfway through. Yes, we would have to go to a replay.

6

ACTION REPLAY:
TRIAL TWO

The atmosphere for the second trial was completely different. We had a new judge, Mr Justice McCullough, who imposed an iron will on the proceedings from the outset.

I imagine the court had been put on notice when the judge asked the CPS if arrangements had been made to separate the defendants from the jurors in the court buildings. He was obviously referring to occasions in the first trial when members of the jury had been forced to sit at tables near to the defendants in the canteen. It was perfectly harmless, but because the canteen was so small there was nowhere else for them to eat. David Calvert-Smith replied that no such arrangements had been made, so the judge withdrew bail and said the defendants would have lunch in their cells. I found that extraordinary, since they had all been out on bail for two and a half years. But it was the judge's way of stamping his authority on the proceedings and letting everyone know that this was a serious criminal case and no levity would be allowed this time.

In the lunch break I decided to take my lunch with the defendants in the cells and arranged for sandwiches, chocolate and drinks
to be brought in. I think it was Bruce Grobbelaar who said: 'Mel,
it is noted that you are the only lawyer here.' Thereafter bail was
renewed but the court made strict arrangements to keep the jury
apart from the defence. The defence had to arrive at court and
sign in every day one hour before the court sat. The jury were
told to come in half an hour later, so that the two groups never
met.

These arrangements meant that each day I would meet Hans
and take him to the court to sign in at the cells. Obviously we got
to know the security staff well and we used to joke that it was
just another autograph-signing session for Hans, who was usually
the first to sign in each day. At lunch, the defendants were not
allowed to leave the building, unlike at the first trial, in case they
bumped into a jury member in the street. The jury then left the
court building before the defendants at the end of every day.

Being cross-examined in court is a stressful experience, and even
more so in a case like this, but I felt that Hans grew in confidence
during the first trial and by the second trial he was a lot more
relaxed and presented his evidence with greater poise and
authority. Each individual's evidence was crucial to the outcome
of the case. This was, after all, a conspiracy charge and the problem
was that if one person went down, he might drag the others down
with him.

Although the evidence was more or less similar in the second
trial, Hans had a greater task because some of the points he raised
in the first trial, such as his business connections with a Mr
Thuys in Holland, relating to the selling of ties, were challenged
by the prosecution in the second trial. They brought Mr Thuys
over from Holland to court specifically to deal with allegations
which were made first time around.

Before the start of the second trial, the CPS thought that by
producing Mr Thuys they would win and initially opposed Hans's
application to go abroad just before the trial began. However,
Desmond de Silva attacked Mr Thuys very successfully and, after

he had finished giving evidence, Desmond was quite satisfied that Thuys had done little or no damage to our case.

In the first trial Hans had revealed that some of the money in his Swiss bank account had come from the sale of ties. Mr Thuys denied paying Hans as much as he had said. When he was called to give evidence in the second trial we showed that we were not avoiding him, quite the opposite. We, in fact, subpoenaed him to attend. When cross-examined he revealed that he did in fact owe Hans money. So, far from being a key prosecution witness, we turned the situation around to our own benefit to disprove the prosecution allegations.

Members of the jury at the first trial found it so interesting that one of them even turned up in the spectators' gallery at the second trial. The judge put a stop to that, although how he found out I do not know.

I received a strange phone call on my mobile towards the end of the second trial from an unknown person, apparently Scottish, who told me it was in my and my client's interests to meet him. I do not know how he got hold of my mobile phone number, which is private. I would only have been interested in meeting him if he were in a position to supply some new evidence which might have been beneficial. However, he just kept on saying that it was in my client's interests to meet him. I repeated this information to Hans and, after checking with Desmond, we took the view that we should not touch this person with a bargepole. Apparently he had earlier approached another party in the case, and he did in fact travel to Winchester. Because he was unable to supply any useful evidence, no further steps were taken.

The fact that this person was willing to travel to Winchester from Scotland at his own expense made me suspect that he was involved in jury-tampering on a professional scale. No sums of money were mentioned and I wanted to report the matter to the police. However, the individual concerned never gave me an address or contact number and always insisted on phoning me. So, unfortunately, I had no information to give the police.

What I suspect these kind of people do is to scan the press and locate cases where they think a defendant might have a bit of money and a conviction is a strong possibility. I imagine they would then pick on a weak-looking member of the jury and perhaps follow that person home. They would then make them an offer of money to attempt to influence the outcome of the case. I have no evidence that this is what that person had in mind, but I doubt whether he went to the trouble of getting my personal and private numbers, and flying down at his own expense, just because he liked my face. I know we made the right decision in having nothing to do with him.

Jerome Lynch, representing Richard Lim, cleverly reiterated a number of holes in the prosecution case and used a number of footballing similes to get his points across to the jury, who were again down to eleven in number, this time because of a family bereavement.

'You may think,' he began, 'whether by accident or design, that in a case about football it is entirely appropriate that you should be reduced to eleven, that you should emerge from a tunnel down there and sit in terraces. You may think it an odd coincidence that exactly the same thing happened at the last trial. The only inference that you can draw from that is that, if there were not coincidences that happen to all of us on a regular basis, there would not be a word for it in the first place.

'We, too, were eleven until Mr Burke lost his partner before the case started. During the trial I wondered what positions we might have played in as we sat here through these weeks. I rather saw Mr Calvert-Smith as the centre-forward, never entirely sure of how he would strike at the goal, unable to make up his mind whether to lob, bang it in with power or to stick to the set-pieces.

'Mr Klevan would be in goal. He has the immediate advantage of – shall I put it – narrowing the angle. He has the ability to wrong-foot anyone, even the referee in this case. Mr de Silva – he was another candidate for the goal, I am bound to say – but I put him in central midfield, a stalwart of the team, playing the game as it was played in those halcyon days back in 1966.

'Mr Burke, he plays on the right because he believes that he always is. And me, I am on the left, not because it is my inclination, but it seems to be where all the yellow cards are picked up, and I am collecting them at the moment. The judge is, of course, the referee, ensuring fair play, applying the rules to the case.

'There has been some levity in this trial, which has been a relief in some way to all of us. Forgive us if we have sought to make light on occasion of what is, after all, a serious case. This is our workplace. You are here for these weeks and I suspect that once you have completed your task here, the chances are it may be many years, if ever, that you will be called for jury service again. We, on the other hand, are perhaps in these courts all the time, and a little levity assists us in the same way I am sure it does in your workplaces.

'Do not be misled into thinking that this is anything other than serious for these four men in the dock. This is a serious case alleging corruption, with serious consequences in a number of respects for all of them.

'One question you will ask yourselves is: would Mr Lim have risked everything that he holds dear? I suppose that is true of all the defendants. He is, as you have heard, of good character; he has never been in any trouble anywhere in the world. He is married to Cora and they want a family. He is guardian to a number of children studying here from the Far East. He spent years building business contacts with the richest and most influential people in the Far East. Royalty, politicians, businessmen have all been those which we know from the evidence – uncontested – he has been associated with.

'His abiding passion has been football. In keeping with his co-defendants, and in particular with Fashanu, it gave him an identity and a pride. He does not, does he, just discard it with a corruption that rocks its very foundation?'

Lynch dealt with the vexing question of how any individual might suddenly contemplate asking some of football's leading professional players to start throwing matches in return for money.

'How on earth does one broach the subject? How would you say, I mean, how do you get to the point of saying to John Fashanu, the star player, England-capped and Gladiators host since 1992 and a businessman, how do you say to him, "Do you think you could get football friends and colleagues of yours to throw a match for me?" I mean, how do you just broach the subject in that way?

'How do you say to Bruce Grobbelaar, one of the world's best goalkeepers over these past years, who on my calculations at any rate seems to have played something up to 700 games for club and country, "Let in the odd goal for 40 grand?"? You would just have no conception of what the response might be, and it seems, you may think, to be far-fetched just to get to that point. The same, of course, applies to Mr Segers.

'These are men not just of good character in the sense that they have not got any criminal convictions. They are men who have devoted their lives to the game, regarded as being among the best. They have also used their fame and wealth to help others less fortunate than themselves.' He was referring to Grobbelaar's counselling of bereaved families after the Hillsborough disaster, and Fashanu's support for relatives of the Zambian national team who died in the air crash.

Lynch also rebuffed police claims that death threats had been issued to Hans Segers and the other defendants in a bid to force them to comply with the wishes of the so-called gambling syndicate: 'I just want to deal with the suggestion of any adverse influence being brought to bear, or any con-trick being exercised. At the outset of the police enquiry, when they questioned Mr Segers, they suggested to him that he may have been threatened to take part in this scheme, suggesting that he might have personal injury if he did not, or even death might result.

'They went that far. The prosecution suggested that perhaps pressure had been brought to bear on Mr Segers by Mr Lim and that he was prepared to agree to anything that I put in cross-examination of Mr Segers. Indeed, when I asked Mr Segers if he had ever been threatened by Mr Lim or any such thing, the judge said, "Well, he couldn't say anything else, could he, because if he *is* being threatened, he is highly unlikely to say yes to that question."

'Similar suggestions were made to Mr Grobbelaar. Neither Mr Segers nor Mr Grobbelaar agreed with such a spurious suggestion. They utterly rejected it. It might have provided them with a defence. Neither was prepared to run the line of, "Well, I took the money offered by Mr Lim to throw a match but I never had the intention of doing so. If he was stupid enough to give me the money, I was going to take it and say thank you very much and do nothing to throw a match."

'Neither of them has proffered that as a defence, which it might well have provided them with. There is not a scrap of evidence to suggest that Mr Lim exercised any adverse influence over these men or that they conned him into parting with his money. Neither Mr Grobbelaar nor Mr Segers holds any brief for Mr Lim; they do not have to protect him at the expense of their own skins.'

Lynch analysed the matches where Hans Segers and Bruce Grobbelaar were alleged by the prosecution to have attempted to rig the results: 'Mr Calvert-Smith says that we cannot point to any specific match where the goalkeepers did anything to throw it or affect its result. He used that phrase we have heard now several times: "It does not matter whether the result owes little, all or nothing to the efforts of Segers or Grobbelaar."

'But are the paymasters going to continue to make substantial payments to these goalkeepers if they are not seen, at the very least, to be doing their best at letting in the odd goal or two so that the result is as desired? I cross-examined Mr Segers about two matches that were specifically put to Mr Lim as having been attempted to be fixed by him. You will remember the Leeds v Wimbledon match, won 4-0 by Leeds, and Newcastle v Wimbledon, also 4-0, on 2 October and 30 October of 1993. Of course, both were substantial losses for Wimbledon and anyone betting on them to lose would have been delighted. But take, for example, the Newcastle game. Mr Lim was at that match, it seems from the telephone evidence.

'Substantial sums must have been wagered in Indonesia. In the first half, Mr Segers makes two impressive saves before a goal is scored. Later in the first half, one of his own team-mates concedes a penalty, which was dispatched with its usual vigour by Mr Beardsley. The score at half-time was 1-0 to Newcastle. That, we would suggest, would be a huge risk to take if Mr Segers is supposed to be throwing this match; to have left it, after the first half, having made two good saves on anyone's view, and then to have conceded a goal only by virtue of a penalty. It seems, you may think, to be something of a risk. There is no guarantee that there is even going to be a shot on goal in the second half.'

Lynch then went into great detail about the five matches Grobbelaar was alleged to have thrown. The only problem was, to follow the prosecution line, if he was trying to throw matches, he was so useless at it that it would have cost the so-called syndicate huge sums of money!

Trevor Burke, addressing the jury on behalf of John Fashanu, said his client was able to negotiate such attractive financial terms with Wimbledon that he did not even have to train with the rest of the squad. Burke told the jury: 'The prosecution bring this case against John Fashanu and the prosecution take upon themselves the burden of proving his guilt. Rest assured, John Fashanu does not wish to be here – he would rather be in Birmingham filming *Gladiators*, but he cannot be, because the law requires him to be here. He is here because the prosecution have brought him here.

'The prosecution take upon themselves a very heavy burden when they accuse anyone of a crime, especially a very serious crime such as this, and the Crown must prove to each and every one of you, so that you are satisfied beyond reasonable doubt, that John Fashanu is guilty as charged.

'The Crown have chosen to allege in two counts on this indictment that John Fashanu is part of a match-fixing conspiracy involving the throwing of Premier Division football matches. We know that during the relevant period, John Fashanu was a striker for both Wimbledon and, more lately, Aston Villa, both Premier Division clubs. During his stay at Wimbledon, he played 272 League games. He scored 106 goals. He was the leading goalscorer for six consecutive seasons up to the end of the 1992 season. Indeed, at the end of the 1992 season, almost bang in the middle of this alleged conspiracy, John Fashanu was the second highest goal-scorer in the Football League. Quite an achievement.

'He was the longest-serving captain of Wimbledon, part of the team that beat the mighty Liverpool in 1988 at Wembley when they secured the FA Cup. He was capped twice for his country. This is a tremendous honour for a footballer. In particular for a young black man, raised in a Dr Barnardo's home, to be capped twice for his country. You may think he can be rightly proud of that. During the period alleged to be the conspiracy, the season of 1993–4, Wimbledon finished in the top six of the Premier Division, the highest position reached in the history of this modest club.

'In 1994, John Fashanu notified the management and the board of directors at Wimbledon that he did not wish to renew his contract with the club as he was proposing, at the age of thirty-one, to retire from professional football to pursue a business career. Not because of injury, not because the management of Wimbledon had lost faith in him or he was only playing in the reserves; not at all. Many would say he was at the peak of his professional football career, but he wished to give it up to pursue actively his full-time business interests.

'In that season he had grossed £193,000. Despite that pay cheque, which would, of course, have been repeated the following year, he wanted to walk away from it. If he is guilty as charged, it is almost inexplicable that in the middle of this lucrative conspiracy to corrupt Premier Division football, his express desire was to retire and remove himself from the opportunity to associate with fellow professionals, whether they be goalkeepers or anybody else, and recruit them to this dishonest enterprise. Because that is the very task the Crown ascribe to John Fashanu, as a fixer and a middle man, recruiting fellow professionals to corrupt the game.

'John Fashanu, uniquely, it would appear, was able to negotiate particularly attractive terms from his then employer Wimbledon. He did not even have to train with the rest of the squad. We have heard some evidence from Mr Segers, and other professional footballers who gave evidence, that when they are not playing on a Saturday or a Wednesday, they spend some considerable time in the week practising their various skills. Not John Fashanu. He did not have to. Wimbledon were perfectly happy to accommodate him. As long as he kept his boots in the back of a car and turned up on a Saturday at about 2.55 pm, kicked the ball about for ninety minutes, Wimbledon were perfectly happy with him. All he had to do to comply with the terms of his contract was to keep himself fit, turn up and play, and do his best to score goals.

'But even that was interrupting his busy business schedule so much that, despite the handsome reward he received, he would still find it more convenient to retire. It may give you some insight as to how successful Mr Fashanu's business empire must have been that playing football for a few hours a week for a salary of almost £200,000 imposed too much of an inconvenience to him.

'We also know that in the summer of 1994, John Fashanu was acting as a TV presenter for the BBC at the World Cup finals in America, as, we discovered, was Ron Atkinson, the then manager of Aston Villa. Shortly after their return to the United Kingdom, Mr Fashanu called Ron Atkinson to discuss the Nigerian international Daniel Amokachi, in his role as a business agent. In Mr Fashanu's diary, seized by police, there are details of a number of other clubs linked by him with Amokachi: Middlesbrough, Wolves, Birmingham, Watford and Brentford. It was quite clear that John Fashanu was trying to broker a transfer by Mr Amokachi to Aston Villa. Mr Atkinson, for whatever reason, rejected the approach. At that time he was not interested in signing this particular player. Unsolicited by John Fashanu, Mr Atkinson made it plain: "If you are available I would like to sign *you*."

'Mr Fashanu had already made his future intentions plain to his then employer, Wimbledon. He was hoping at the end of his contract to retire. But as a result of a telephone conversation with Mr Atkinson in the summer of that year, he discovers that Aston Villa are willing to pay £1.35 million to secure his services.

'In due course he negotiated his transfer so that he would be paid a signing-on fee of £200,000, and you can see from the diary entry that Mr Fashanu is clearly sketching his bonuses, his match appearances and his various fees, and it is clear that for the two-year contract he signed to play for Aston Villa he had the potential to make a minimum of £532,000, and if he scored 20 goals in each season he could add a further £50,000 to it. This is a very considerable contract. It is hardly surprising, you may think, that it was easy for him to walk away from £193,000, but the figures on offer from Aston Villa really put a different complexion on it.

'He imposed, and Aston Villa accepted, similar conditions to those he had been able to negotiate with Wimbledon, that he would be able to travel to Africa, if appropriate notice was given, and that he would have time off at the beginning of the season to comply with his London Weekend Television contract to film *Gladiators*.

'Aston Villa accepted his terms and the contract was signed. We know that soon after signing for Aston Villa, he went to Rwanda and then took the appropriate time to film *Gladiators* in Birmingham.

'We know that John Fashanu played football for Aston Villa as a striker between August 1994 and the end of his career on 4 February 1995. He played sixteen matches for them in both the League and various Cup ties before Ryan Giggs tackled him in a game against Manchester United and damaged his knee, such that the specialists employed by Aston Villa advised that it was the end of his professional career.

'On receipt of medical advice, an insurance premium was payable by Aston Villa. They were satisfied his career was over. During those sixteen matches Aston Villa won six, drew six and lost only four. Mr Atkinson, who, during his long career in football, has managed some of the great teams both here and abroad, was able to say without hesitation: "John Fashanu gave 100 per cent in every match he played for my club." '

Burke highlighted the fact that one of Fashanu's early games for Villa was against Southampton: 'If the Crown are right in the assertions they make in this trial, this, you may think, was an ideal opportunity for the Indonesians to unlawfully enrich themselves. Both of their allegedly corrupted players had recently moved clubs.

Mr Grobbelaar had signed for Southampton and Mr Fashanu for Aston Villa. What a perfect opportunity to make money. You have a gifted centre-forward who can score goals and a corrupt goal-keeper who, for money, will let them in. This is the perfect match to fix. We know it took place on 24 August 1994. However, there was no telephone contact between any of the defendants from 13 May to 13 September.

'If the Crown are accurate in the assertions they make, you may think there would have been a considerable amount of telephone contact, perhaps directly to Mr Fashanu receiving his instructions, and perhaps by Richard Lim to Mr Grobbelaar, or both of them, dictating the result required by the money men in Indonesia. They would not have missed the opportunity, would they, if these men are guilty? But we know there was not a single telephone call, or a single bank transfer, or any other shred of evidence that Mr Calvert-Smith could lay before you in the hope that you would accept it as proof positive of corrupt football. Mr Calvert-Smith would have mentioned it to you at every opportunity.

'The Crown do not suggest that John Fashanu himself threw any match by any activity or lack of it on the field of play. That is now abundantly clear in the evidence in this case. He is prosecuted on the basis that he is a middle man, a fixer, not a player who throws a match himself. It is totally preposterous that in any given game we have John Fashanu as the centre-forward for Wimbledon, giving 100 per cent in a match, and behind him is a goalkeeper recruited by Fashanu expressly to throw the game. What a totally incon-sistent allegation for the Crown to maintain, but they maintain it. It takes only a moment to consider it to appreciate how ridiculous a proposition that is.'

Burke also revealed that on 1 December, 14 December and 28 December 1993, Liverpool played Wimbledon three times and all three footballers in the dock appeared in the matches. 'The first finished 1-1, the second 2-2 and the third 1-1, with Fashanu scoring the goal. Again, the Crown's telephone schedules revealed no contact between 26 November and 17 December, a period covering two of the three matches when, if one was to believe in a conspiracy theory, one would have expected a regular flow of telephone calls to have been made.'

Much of the prosecution's evidence concerned payments made to a number of bank accounts controlled by Fashanu, who could prove that payments from the Far East were concerned with the development of a duty-free shop at Lagos Airport in Nigeria, funded by Johannes Josef, and nothing to do with football matters. In fact, these payments continued long after the alleged conspiracy was said to have dried up following the publication of the match-fixing stories in *The Sun*.

Fashanu and Josef had met in March 1991 when Mr Josef visited London and stayed at the Dorchester Hotel. Josef was in urgent need of dental treatment and Lim turned to Fashanu for help. Fashanu duly made the necessary introductions for Josef to see a dentist and later, with Lim acting as interpreter, the two men began to discuss business. One of Mr Josef's interests was as a commodity broker dealing with cocoa and at that stage Fashanu was dating Melissa Kassa Mapsi, whose uncle was the president of the Ivory Coast, which is the world's largest producer of cocoa.

As the evidence unfolded, Burke was successfully steering the minds of the jury away from footballing matters and towards Fashanu's rapidly expanding business empire, although football, obviously, was forming a significant part of that empire.

Burke explained that Fashanu and Grobbelaar both made frequent appearances on the South African TV station M-Net, and that Fashanu wished to recruit Grobbelaar to scout for promising players in Zimbabwe, for whom Grobbelaar was goalkeeper and assistant coach. Burke explained that in one particular meeting the two could not agree terms, because Grobbelaar wished to have the comfort of a salary rather than a commission on any deals with him fronting up his own expenses. Fashanu frequently brought African players over to England to train with Wimbledon, even if he himself wasn't always joining in the training! Ironically, Grobbelaar had also spoken to Fashanu about investing in the Mondoro safari park project. Fashanu, according to Grobbelaar, was the richest African he knew.

Burke also revealed the wealth enjoyed by Fashanu's in-laws. Melissa's family maintain property in the south of France, the Bahamas, New York, Ivory Coast, Gabon and Switzerland. As well as her uncle being president of the Ivory Coast, her aunt is the empress of the Central African Republic. Her father is a distinguished politician and an extremely wealthy businessman. The dowry for their marriage was £200,000, with a further £100,000 gift from the father towards buying a house. During the course of their relationship, Melissa has introduced John to the presidents of Zambia, Gabon, Nigeria, Ghana, Sierra Leone and South Africa.

Yes, even Nelson Mandela's name was used in the course of justice at Winchester Crown Court.

7

VINCENT THE VIPER

Chris Vincent was absolutely crucified when he appeared in the witness box. In all of my years in the legal profession I have never seen anyone so totally discredited in front of a judge and jury. Both in his cross-examination of Vincent and in his closing speech, Rodney Klevan, defending Bruce Grobbelaar, tore into Vincent and ripped his credibility to shreds.

Klevan said: 'This case is about a group of heroes and one villain. Villains abound all over and always have. They are in reality and they thrive in the world of fiction. But Christopher Vincent is in our submission, the repository of treachery. He is a serpent. No creator of literature could have invented him. He slithers forward to his riches, hoping you will do right by him.

'He does not care for truth or justice. He cares for only two things, himself and money, and the more money he can get out of this trial the better. He is no one's hero. Vincent is a liar without equal whose evidence must be totally rejected. He is a man who has corrupted this trial from beginning to end.

'To Vincent, friendship is a disposable commodity. If it can be sold in the market place, it will be sold. If a man can be destroyed for his purposes, he will be destroyed.'

Klevan described Grobbelaar as a football giant, a fierce competitor and a man of good character. He said that Grobbelaar and Vincent were very different personalities. He said that a succession of witnesses had portrayed Grobbelaar as a generous, open-handed, open-hearted man, a giver, not a taker. He had willingly donated time and money to a variety of well-respected causes. Indeed, after the Hillsborough tragedy, Grobbelaar attended many of the supporters' funerals and had counselled bereaved families. Former team-mates had also appeared in court to voice their opinion that Grobbelaar was a talented and respected professional and not the sort of player to throw matches. 'These are the crucial professionals,' said Rodney. 'If they say they did not see anything untoward happening, then nothing untoward did happen.'

Klevan added: 'I would describe Vincent as a commercial pimp, a con-man, a bankrupt, a man whose own father wants nothing to do with him and rejects him. That was the evidence. His own brother is at odds with him. A man who turns on a friend without a moment's compunction, we say without true reason or explanation he strikes. Cross Vincent and he will destroy you. Mr Grobbelaar gave Vincent everything, his time, his name, his money, his friendship, and in return has received treachery and, more importantly – and this I do invite you to consider, please, and carry with you – he has received in return lies. That is the critical feature here. Vincent has lied.'

Klevan went on: 'You will recollect that he had taken Mr Grobbelaar's money for Mondoro under the masquerade that it would be properly and decently applied within the business. You will recollect, at that time he had not told Mr Grobbelaar of his bankruptcy or in fact, if that was not known to him, of the debts that were multiplying in the County Court. You will recollect, no money paid back to people to whom he owed it.

'I asked him, did he tell Mr Grobbelaar of the failed businesses? No.

'Did you tell him in the months that followed in that year about the various County Court judgments that were mounting against you?'

'No, sir, I did not.'

'And I went through the amounts: "You were cultivating the friendship and obtaining the money of Mr Grobbelaar while people were obtaining judgments against you in the local County Court, was that right?"

'Correct, sir.'

'This man just left such a trail of debts. He says it is other people's money, it is not his. None of them was repaid. I asked him: "Were you being selective in what you told Mr Grobbelaar?" '

'Yes, sir.'

'You wanted to gain his interest, is that right?'

'Correct.'

'His friendship?'

'Correct.'

'His money?'

'Correct.'

'And to give the appearance of being a successful businessman?'

'Correct.'

'You were hardly open and frank with him even from the beginning, were you?'

'Correct.'

'Even by the answers of this man and the directness of them, he seems to take pride in his villainy. He has not got an ounce of shame. On one or two matters that were really difficult for him he tried, but then the reality of it: he set about to con Mr Grobbelaar from the outset. Whatever he says or does must be measured by one thing: what is in it for Vincent?'

Grobbelaar denied corruptly accepting £2,000 from Vincent, who had told the former Liverpool goalkeeper that he had launched a new gambling syndicate. Their discussions were secretly filmed and the prosecution claimed that Grobbelaar had willingly accepted the 'gift' from Vincent and had admitted on tape to throwing earlier matches. Vincent claimed that he had approached Grobbelaar to take bribes so that he could repay him for the money he had invested in the safari business.

Grobbelaar was also accused of receiving £40,000 for throwing a match against Newcastle in November 1993 and attempting to influence the result of four other games. The prosecution further alleged that Grobbelaar had lost a £125,000 bonus when he instinctively made two superb saves after deliberately diving the wrong way in the match against Manchester United which ended 3-3. But nothing of this sort was borne out by videos of the match, said Klevan.

Klevan explained that in the video-taped meeting with Vincent, Grobbelaar had concocted stories about match-fixing in a bid to discover who Vincent was working for. 'Nothing that was said was meant to be a truthful admission of his conduct,' Klevan said. 'He appreciates he should have acted in a different way. Any talk of throwing games is stupid and dangerous and that is why he is here today.'

Klevan detailed Vincent's former business failures, which he had concealed from Grobbelaar before persuading him to invest in the Mondoro venture. Klevan expressed surprise that the Crown were relying so heavily on Vincent's evidence. He told the jury: 'They know he is tarnished beyond measure but they still, because it suits their purposes, want you to rely on him. There is no evidence to suggest that Grobbelaar tried to throw matches.'

We knew that Vincent was planning to write a book and had received a healthy advance payment from the publishers, Macmillan, plus sums of money from other media sources. Klevan reminded the jury that Vincent stood to gain financially from any convictions in the trial. He said: 'Payments to any witnesses in a trial may cause a witness to exaggerate, distort or withhold their account, or tell lies. The cause of justice is deeply affected by payments.

'Mr Vincent is an odious mercenary. He is avaricious beyond measure. He is a witness on contract. He might as well have taken the oath on a chequebook.

'I am aware that Vincent is not on trial, and if he benefits by a finding against Grobbelaar – the man he admits he tried to destroy – so be it. If he makes his money, so be it. If that is the inevitable consequence of your verdict, so be it. But, and it is a very heavy but, please make sure you get it right before that man Vincent triumphs in the wake of your verdict.'

8

DESMOND'S LATE STRIKE

The second trial was almost an action replay of the first. Much of the evidence was duplicated and as a result, the media took less and less interest as the weeks went by. But their interest was rekindled as the trial neared its conclusion, and we wondered what the result would be after so much hard work had been put in to see that justice was done for our client.

Desmond de Silva's closing speech on Hans's behalf was a masterpiece. Powerful, carefully thought out, and delivered in clear, precise tones. There was no room for misunderstanding. He used every available advantage open to him. He made no excuses for the mistakes Hans had obviously made when answering police questions. He pointed out the flaws in the prosecution's arguments. And he firmly stressed Hans's qualities as a brave, fearless and honest goalkeeper who was valued highly by his employers.

Where his client had told a pack of lies, as happened in this case, Desmond said so quite simply. No attempt was made to pull the wool over the eyes of the jury. However, when something needed explaining, perhaps a hidden reason, he would clarify. The circumstances surrounding Hans's association with Mr Thuys and details of his Swiss bank account needed explaining, and Desmond dealt admirably with these aspects of the case.

Where football knowledge was needed, he simply relied on the expert evidence of others, notably Bob Wilson, not forgetting points from the undisclosed material. This is a legal term for Crown evidence which was not used but to which we had access (every word of which he had read). He reminded the jury that the prosecution had consulted the FA, who asked for the views of Jimmy Armfield, a respected ex-international player and radio broadcaster on the goals being investigated, but nothing untoward was found – and that was from the Crown's own evidence.

Desmond never lost sight of the human factor, the common touch with a wicked sense of humour. If I had to choose a counsel to defend me on a murder charge (at the moment I have no one in mind but circumstances might change), I would want Desmond in my corner. There are many fine advocates, but to coin an Alan Hansenism, Desmond is 'the business'.

It would take up too much space to go through the whole of the second trial, but I would like to record the highlights of Desmond's closing speech.

Hans, if found guilty, was almost certainly facing a prison sentence. A powerful case had been presented by the prosecution. They attempted to link lists of alleged telephone calls between the defendants, on or around the dates of certain matches, with details of deposits of sums of money being paid into various bank accounts.

Much of their evidence, however, came from discredited witnesses such as Chris Vincent – who sold his soul to the devil, and to *The Sun* – and Dutch businessman Frans Thuys, who owed Hans large sums of money from the ties venture.

Desmond's closing speech to the jury was a marvellous example of courtroom oratory. Read on and you will understand why.

Friday, 25 July 1997: Closing speech on behalf of Hans Segers by Desmond de Silva QC

Members of the jury, it falls for me now to address you on behalf of Mr Hans Segers, the man whom I have been privileged to represent over these many weeks before you.

You have heard two speeches against Mr Segers from my learned friend, Mr Calvert-Smith.

This is the one and only speech I shall be making to you on behalf of Mr Segers, and I make it at the end of the case. I make it in the hope that I can put together, for your assistance, all the matters which we hope will be worthy of your consideration when you come to determine issues of guilt and innocence.

What I would first say to you is this: Be careful about the prosecution theory of patterns of telephone calls surrounding Wimbledon matches. These calls occurred whether Wimbledon lost, drew, won, and, even more significantly, when Wimbledon were not even playing, and even when the English football season was over. There is strong evidence that many of these calls refer to Dutch matches.

Secondly, Mr Segers was paid. He was paid to do something perfectly legal. He was paid to do forecasting. As to the FA rules, I shall deal with those later.

The fixing of games, or the forecasting of results? The throwing of matches, or the forecasting of their outcome? These are the issues that lie at the heart of this case.

We know that Mr Grobbelaar, many years ago, way back in 1986, was forecasting for a Norwegian newspaper. You know that. Undisputed evidence.

We know from a Dutch magazine, the name of which I will not seek to pronounce, that forecasting is done in Holland.

We now know that Mr Fashanu broadcast to South Africa on something called the M-Net. And what did he do in those broadcasts?

He was predicting or forecasting matches, for which he was being paid, if my memory serves me right, some £25,000. Most of these forecasts, anyway, were the work of a Mr Ian Wilson – you heard Mr Wilson give evidence – but the information went out in the name of, and in the knowledge of, Mr Fashanu. For £25,000. From which you may conclude that there is good money to be made in forecasting.

We now say to you, on behalf of Mr Segers: Here he is, an exceptional Dutch player, playing in England, according to Bob Wilson, with 'the fastest feet in the business'.

Broadcasting to Holland, as he did. Undisputed. Using his knowledge and experience, he says, to forecast Dutch results for those in a former Dutch colony who were brought up in the culture of Dutch football.

And forecasts going out, he believed, or you may conclude, to a substantial Chinese population in Indonesia and Malaysia. As we all know, Chinese enthusiasm for gambling is legendary.

It is not disputed that there was Mr Segers sitting indoors with a satellite decoder, apparatus for watching Dutch football and being able to watch Dutch Teletext, which gave information up to the point of the match almost, of injuries and the like that could affect the outcome of the game.

That is all undisputed evidence, that he had the ability to tap into this information.

The important thing in this case is that the prosecution do not say that there was no forecasting. What they do say is that forecasting turned into something else. Into something corrupt.

They concede, as my learned friend Mr Calvert-Smith did in his final speech, 'Yes, there may well have been forecasting. We say it was a stepping stone to something else.'

But supposing, in the case of Mr Segers, it did not go on to anything else? Supposing he just stuck to that forecasting?

You see how unjust it could become to look at those telephone calls and say, oh well, this means corruption.

Thirdly, ladies and gentlemen, there is not one shred of positive evidence that Mr Segers has ever thrown a match or ever attempted to throw a match.

What is the position on the evidence we have heard?

We know that in early 1996, the prosecution sent a number of videos of Wimbledon matches to the Football Association. Mr Jimmy Armfield, that well-known figure in football and former England captain, who is with the FA, was required to analyse those games to see if there was anything untoward about them.

That evidence was read to you and you know that he scrutinized those matches for over a week, it seems, and the results have been read to you. Nothing untoward – and that was the prosecution expert.

You also heard from Mr Bob Wilson, who also looked at a large number of matches. Nothing untoward. Some matches were examined not only by Mr Bob Wilson but also by Mr Armfield. Nothing untoward.

You, ladies and gentlemen of the jury, have a chart of Wimbledon matches, and I just want to pinpoint all the matches that have been viewed either by one or both experts.

The first match which was scrutinized by Mr Bob Wilson was the match of 24 August 1993, the Sheffield United versus Wimbledon match. Nothing untoward.

The next match that was lost by Wimbledon was on 2 October 1993, Leeds United versus Wimbledon. Again, Bob Wilson viewed that. Nothing untoward.

Then we go down to the third match which was lost by Wimbledon, on 25 October 1993. Wimbledon versus Ipswich. Bob Wilson. Nothing untoward.

Then we go down to 30 October 1993. Newcastle versus Wimbledon. Bob Wilson. Nothing untoward. Then, ladies and gentlemen, we notice the match on 26 December, Wimbledon versus Coventry. There is no video now. So that, of course, has not been witnessed.

Nor the match of 20 November, Manchester United versus Wimbledon, where there is no video.

We then go down to 1994. 1 January, Wimbledon versus Arsenal. Bob Wilson. Nothing untoward.

We then go to where the other video exists. 5 February 1994,

Blackburn versus Wimbledon. Bob Wilson and Armfield viewed that video. Nothing untoward. Both experts did that.

We then, ladies and gentlemen, go on to 26 February, Southampton versus Wimbledon. Bob Wilson and Armfield. Nothing untoward.

We go to 16 March 1994, Chelsea versus Wimbledon. I believe that was Bob Wilson. Nothing untoward.

We then go down to 7 May, Everton versus Wimbledon. Bob Wilson and Jimmy Armfield viewed that. Nothing untoward.

We then go to 1994-5 season, 1 October, Wimbledon versus Tottenham. Bob Wilson. Nothing untoward.

We turn to 8 October, Wimbledon versus Arsenal. Bob Wilson. Nothing untoward.

We go to 17 October, Nottingham Forest versus Wimbledon. Bob Wilson and Armfield viewed that. Nothing untoward.

We then go to 22 October 1994, Liverpool versus Wimbledon. Bob Wilson. Nothing untoward.

So, ladies and gentlemen, you should get a clear picture of what our case is. That is, ninety-five per cent of all the matches Wimbledon lost have been viewed by one or other and sometimes both experts, and all the evidence is one way. Nothing untoward.

Add to those experts, Jimmy Armfield and Bob Wilson, the fact that Mr Joe Kinnear, who was the manager of Wimbledon, reviewed and scrutinized videos of all Wimbledon matches.

Apart from the fact that he would be there watching the match, Mr Kinnear continued to pick Mr Segers to play in goal for Wimbledon. You can conclude from this, can you not, he, Mr Kinnear, that eminent manager, never lost his confidence in Mr Segers?

Nor did Mr Segers lose the confidence of his club and week in, week out, at home or away, come rain or come shine, Mr Segers had been picked time and time and time again to continue to keep goal for Wimbledon.

So it comes as no surprise to you, I suppose, when the prosecution is driven to concede that they cannot point to a single incident in any match that shows that Mr Segers did throw or attempt to throw any match.

That is powerful evidence, members of the jury, when you look at it in the round. Segers was picked and picked again until injury struck him down in 1995.

Can I invite you to look at a list of 1995–6 match facts concerning Wimbledon results. This is the time Hans Segers was injured.

Between 16 September and 23 December 1995, Wimbledon played fourteen matches without Mr Segers.

They lost seven matches on the trot, one after the other. Seven consecutive losses. Can you imagine what my learned friend Mr Calvert-Smith would have said if Mr Segers was playing?

Wimbledon, without Mr Segers, lost nine and drew five matches without a single win.

Victory comes back to Wimbledon on 26 December. Segers is back. Wimbledon's first victory for two and a half months, and Segers is back.

Ladies and gentlemen of the jury, the prosecution suggest to you that in the football season 1993–4, Mr Segers was a party to a conspiracy to throw Wimbledon games for money.

The flaw in the prosecution theory is that in the season 1993–4, with a goalkeeper supposed to be cutting matches against his side's interests, Wimbledon enjoyed one of the club's most successful seasons.

The club equalled the finest position they ever achieved in the Premier League. Is that done by the throwing of games?

A goalkeeper, members of the jury, stands between the goalposts and beneath the crossbar. And he stands there alone. He stands between the glory of his side's victory and the misery of relegation. He stands between his side's success and his side's failure.

In 1993–4, as you have heard from one of the witnesses who gave evidence, he was one of the architects of his side's success at Wimbledon in that season.

It is totally and utterly inconsistent with the allegation being made against him by the prosecution, is it not?

It is our submission to you, and I hope you will find favour with it, that Wimbledon's success in 1993–4 cannot be built on some corrupt dealings by Hans Segers. A corruption designed to ensure that his side lost. It just does not hang together.

You do not have to be a genius to work out that Wimbledon did so well in 1993–4 because Hans Segers played his part in saving goals, not throwing them; helping Wimbledon to win victory, and not ensuring defeat.

Hans Segers signed a two-year contract with Wimbledon on 25 March 1994 on the following terms.

The basic salary is £1,000 a week, plus a signing-on fee payable on 1 July 1994 and another payable on 1 July 1995, plus a loyalty bonus payable on 30 June 1995 and another payable on 30 June 1996.

A vastly enhanced contract. When you look at those figures, you realize that he enjoyed the confidence of the club. His success was being recognized in a remarkably dramatic way, and the prosecution theory that he was out there secretly doing his side down for money just does not hold.

No wonder, when Mr Hans Segers was being cross-examined by my learned friend, Mr Calvert-Smith, and Mr Calvert-Smith made to him the suggestion that the Crown is making in this case, Mr Segers became rather emotional and when Mr Calvert-Smith started talking about some match for which a video exists, you will remember Mr Segers's answer: 'Show the jury the video. Show the jury the video and show me what I did wrong.' We did not see any video at that stage.

You only had to look at Mr Hans Segers in that witness box when matters were touched upon in connection with football to realize one thing from his demeanour, that the overriding passion of his professional life was the game he played and the game he loved.

No wonder emotion broke through when he was accused, in effect, of bringing the cancer of corruption into the heart of the national game.

The fourth point, members of the jury, is this. He is not in the dock for telling lies to the police. He is not in the dock for infringing, or possibly infringing, FA rules, and suspicion is not enough.

Accusations, ladies and gentlemen of the jury, are easy to make, but if the prosecution wants you to convict Hans Segers, a man of hitherto unblemished record, what you need from the prosecution is proof, proof, proof. Proof beyond reasonable doubt. We submit that there is no such proof.

The first witness for the prosecution was Mr Christopher Vincent. No doubt you will remember him well. He told you, members of the jury, that he had no dealings with Hans Segers at any time. He never knew Hans Segers, save as a well-known goalkeeper, and he knew nothing else about him that he could add to what he had already said.

Vincent has a clear financial interest in making his story more sensational, and people make stories more sensational by injecting into those stories other well-known names.

In Mr Segers's case, Mr Thuys has a financial interest in these proceedings because he has spotted in these proceedings, in these events, an excuse for avoiding to pay Mr Segers the money to which he is entitled.

There are two things, ladies and gentlemen, I want to say to you about the law. Whatever I say to you about the law in this case is, of course, subject to what my lord (*the judge*) tells you about the law in due course.

My lord will, I have no doubt, tell you that you have got to consider the case of each defendant separately and you have got to give a separate verdict in each case, because the cases against them are somewhat different.

For example, Mr Segers is the only defendant on one charge in this case. There is no suggestion that Mr Segers ever made a confession or anything of that kind.

Come to think of it, it is really quite extraordinary, is it not, that when the prosecution suggest that here was Mr Grobbelaar, a goalkeeper, and here was Mr Segers, both working for the same paymaster, Mr Lim, to do the same things – because that is the suggestion – that throughout this period we are concerned with, Mr Grobbelaar and Mr Segers never even speak to each other?

The prosecution in regard to Count 1, which is the only count in which Mr Segers is named, says to you in opening that there is no direct evidence against Mr Segers. That is absolutely right. The Crown rely on inferences.

I think at an early stage of this trial – it might even have been when my learned friend was opening the case, but certainly when Mr Vincent was in the witness box – you sent a note up to the court saying is there any video in relation to Mr Segers? *Sun*-type video, you will remember, and of course there was not. There is no direct evidence against Mr Segers.

The prosecution say we cannot show which matches were selected for throwing, but we rely on the timings of telephone calls and ask you to draw inferences, and the payments to Mr Segers all follow matches Wimbledon lost.

Ladies and gentlemen, the danger of that theory is this: Even the most successful teams lose matches.

So far as the law is concerned, before you can convict Mr Segers, you have got to be satisfied that there was in existence a conspiracy between two or more people that gifts of money would be corruptly given and corruptly accepted by football players as an inducement or as rewards for improperly influencing or attempting to influence the outcome of football matches.

Secondly, you have to be satisfied so that you are sure that Mr Segers joined such a conspiracy. And thirdly, you would have to be sure that he intended, in return for the money he received, if the opportunity arose, to influence or attempt to influence the outcome of one or more matches. In other words, do his side, Wimbledon, down. The intention is very important. Let me give you an example. Supposing you were a football player and somebody came along to you and said look, here is £50,000. I want you to throw the match next Saturday and you say, jolly good, of course I will for £50,000. You put the money in your pocket, laugh all the way to the bank and have no intention of doing anything of the kind. You simply pocket the money. You would not be a member of a conspiracy. You would not have the intention to give effect to the object of the conspiracy. Have you got me?

So all of those things have got to be proved before you can possibly convict Mr Segers. One, that the conspiracy existed. Two, that he joined it; and three, he intended to give effect to the object of the conspiracy.

There is a vital matter, members of the jury, on which I wish to address you, in case you seek to draw what I am going to consider an unfair inference against Mr Segers because of the way things were put.

You will remember when Mr Segers was in the witness box, and indeed when my learned friend Mr Calvert-Smith came to address you, he asked him for his Swiss bank accounts, you will remember. These are Swiss bank accounts Mr Segers told you were closed in 1995. The RNB account in Switzerland was closed in 1995.

Please remember what Mr Segers said as to why that Swiss account was set up.

He said two things. He said that Swiss account, containing £104,000, was set up for tax reasons – and when he was being interviewed, you may have little doubt that he had the fear of the taxman in mind.

I come now to Mr Thuys, his Dutch partner in a ties business. Some £45,000 of the £104,000 came from forecasting over two seasons. In rough terms, £48,000 from Mr Fashanu. That leaves very little to explain of the £104,000. Mr Segers says that small amount, a figure in the region of £10,000–£11,000, came from Mr Thuys and came in cash.

When his contract ran out with Wimbledon he would have been unemployed, but to get legal aid he had to deposit £30,000, which he has done, and you have seen the document. Mr Segers needed his share of money from the ties business to put down towards legal aid. Indeed, he has had to raise the money by some other way, by selling something else, some bonds.

Let me deal, ladies and gentlemen, with the telephone evidence in this case, upon which the Crown relies. Before I deal with that evidence in detail, can I just, in the briefest outline, tell you what Mr Segers said about his telephone calls with Mr Fashanu.

Firstly, he says, we were friends. We were professional colleagues. He was the captain of Wimbledon. I was the vice-captain. Of course we used to talk on the telephone. One can imagine the sort of things that two men in the same side, captain and vice-captain, would talk about. Tactics. All manner of things. Players and how they were performing, and so on and so forth.

Secondly, Mr Segers told you his wife, Astrid, and Mrs Fashanu, Miss Kassa Mapsi at the time, were friends and used to speak on the telephone. Therefore, you would have a Fashanu telephone ringing a Segers telephone because their wives used to speak. There would be calls, he said, about tickets and ticketing arrangements where tickets were required for matches.

Mr Segers went on to say that when he was about his ties business and was in meetings with people or when he was playing golf – look at his diaries, you will see lots of golfing events – he used to switch his mobile off. Of course, if Mr Lim was trying to get hold of him and could not, Lim, he says, would often leave a message with Fashanu to say if you speak to Segers, please tell him that I want to talk with him, or whatever. So you would get calls for a variety of reasons.

Let us take an example, please, of what the Crown say are back-to-back telephone calls. Let us take an imaginary example on the basis of the evidence given by Mr Segers. Supposing Fashanu rings Mr Segers and says to him, 'By the way, Richard wants to find out whether you have any alterations to a forecast you have given him. He needs to talk to you.' So, having received that telephone call from Mr Fashanu, Mr Segers may ring Mr Lim to say, 'Oh about that forecast. I am not changing them. They are all fine.' Lim, if he is correct, would then say, 'OK, that is excellent.' Then he (*Lim*) would call Mr Lo-Bon-Swe (his contact in Indonesia) and the forecasts are as told to you before. There is no change.

So you see how you can get back-to-back calls as a result of the forecasting. I simply take that as an example, the sort of thing that could happen. So you can see Fashanu ringing Segers, Segers ringing Lim, Lim ringing Lo-Bon-Swe, and it is perfectly explicable within the context of the forecasting that Mr Segers has told you about. So within a few minutes you could have a whole slew of telephone calls which look as if they are back-to-back and there is nothing sinister in that at all.

My learned friend Mr Lynch, in the course of his speech, demonstrated to you that the prosecution patterns of telephone calls equalling the fixing of matches, or the throwing of matches, is a flawed theory, because the pattern tends to be the same whether Wimbledon loses, whether Wimbledon draws, or whether Wimbledon wins.

The pattern is the same.

I need to go a bit further with you, ladies and gentlemen, and give you an example of calls that can only be referable to Dutch matches, if one is logical about it, and the reason is simple: because the Wimbledon season was over.

The telephone calls, therefore, could not possibly have had any reference to the Wimbledon matches. All you need is one or two examples of this to demonstrate that the calls in relation to Mr Segers could be referable to Dutch matches and not English ones. Although, as you will remember, Mr Segers did say from time to time Mr Lim would come to him for a second opinion on a team in England.

The pattern of telephone calls is there when Wimbledon is not playing, and they are only referable, we would submit on any fair-minded view, to Dutch forecasting.

So, ladies and gentlemen, you know one can go through it and through it and through it, but I hope I have done enough to demonstrate to you what I was saying to you before.

The pattern of telephone calls can be the same whether Wimbledon is winning, losing, or drawing, or when Wimbledon is not playing at all, or even when the Wimbledon season has ended. What does that equal?

It is very, very, strong support, is it not, of what Mr Segers says to you? I was forecasting Dutch matches.

Of all the defendants in this case, Mr Segers was the only one,

I think, to give an interview to the police. In that interview, members of the jury, he lied and he lied, and Mr Segers agrees: Yes I did.

But I want to examine the background of that with you for a moment, because prior to November 1994, that is when the Grobbelaar story broke in the newspapers, Mr Segers says to you, in effect, I was forecasting for Lim so as to assist Mr Lim's associates in betting on football matches. That is the effect of his evidence.

In November 1994, the Grobbelaar story breaks in *The Sun* newspaper. Mr Segers has told you that when that happened, there was gossip, there were people ringing him up.

You heard his evidence. I am not going to go through it again. But he got a bit alarmed and he consulted friends and he got concerned about the forecasting that he had been doing for Mr Lim.

Segers says to you, in effect, I got frightened in case I was doing something wrong, and I read the FA rules for the first time in this regard.

Please remember this: he kept saying to Mr Calvert-Smith, who was cross-examining him, 'I am not a lawyer.'

The Football Association's definition of misconduct is as follows: 'In addition to matters referred to in any other rule, it shall be misconduct if any club, director, official, referee, or player is proved to the satisfaction of the council or a commission thereof to have done or permitted or assisted in doing or permitting to bet on any football match other than authorized and registered football pools.'

We are not concerned with football pools in this case, are we? He said when he read that, he felt he had been in breach of the FA rules. He had not had occasion to look at them before. He felt he might be classed as someone who had assisted in betting on any football match, and that is what it says.

Mr Segers told you he came to believe that what he had done might have been contrary to the FA rules. For him to have forecast and therefore assisted in betting on any football match, nothing to do with the pools.

He has told you he knew what happened to a man called Lou Macari and that saga when, as I understand it, that manager, Mr Lou Macari, had bet on his own side to lose.

Well, that is direct betting, you follow. Lou Macari was suspended and as I understand it his team came to be relegated.

Here is Mr Segers saying he knew that would be wrong – and I think you will pick that up in his interview – but he never thought forecasting was wrong until he read the rules.

Whether he has read it correctly or not does not matter, but that is his reading of it. 'Assisting in betting with regard to any football match.' That is how he read it.

When he read those FA rules, he told you, he panicked because he thought what he did might be classed as assisting in betting. He told you that his fears about betting were reinforced when the police came to his home on 14 March 1995 and told him that one of the things they were looking at was defrauding bookmakers.

Can I just invite you to that interview, page two of his interview, members of the jury. Detective Sergeant Mitchell's second question to him, 'You've been arrested for a couple of offences. I will repeat to you again.' Mr Segers says to you, I was told as before: 'Conspiracy to defraud bookmakers and also an offence under the Prevention of Corruption Act.'

Of course, there is no charge in relation to bookmakers, but he had read the FA rules by then and was extremely worried about his own position, assisting in betting on any match, and the police then tell him that one of the things they are looking into is a conspiracy to defraud bookmakers. Even the simplest intellect – I hope he will forgive me for saying that! – even the simplest intellect would understand bookmakers equals gambling, pretty much.

He was the only defendant in this case not to ask for a solicitor before he was interviewed. He was given the opportunity and did not ask for one. Every person, before he is interviewed by the police, is entitled to seek the advice of a solicitor. Mr Segers did not want one, and when he was in the witness box I asked him why?

He said, well, I did not think I had done anything illegal. Of course, but he thought he might have been in breach of the FA rules for forecasting and that it might affect the whole of his life as a footballer; but so far as anything illegal is concerned, he said I did not want a solicitor because I had done nothing illegal. I did not need his advice. So he goes into that interview without the advice, assistance or comfort of a solicitor that he was otherwise entitled to.

Then what does he do? He lies about ever knowing Mr Lim – and I am going to take this in short form. Whichever way the police approached it, he says I do not know Mr Lim, do not know Mr Heng Suan Lim, do not know Mr Richard Lim, never heard of him, never spoken to such a man, do not know of his existence.

Why? Why was he lying?

Well, Mr Segers has told you, because if I admitted to knowing Lim and how I got to know him, it would result in the forecasting coming out. That is the one thing he was trying to avoid and decided to lie about it.

So he could not admit to knowing Mr Lim because the only basis he knew Mr Lim on was the basis of forecasting.

They said, 'Well, what did you do? What did you speak about? What was your business?' And the forecasting comes out and so he lies and lies and lies. He lied about the money, where the money in his Swiss bank account came from.

Why? Because to tell the truth would have meant disclosing that a chunk of that money had come from forecasting and Mr Lim. So we are back to the forecasting, the one thing he had become absolutely petrified of disclosing for fear his career would go up in smoke.

So when it comes to his Swiss account, he lies and comes up with a fantastic story that when he was in his teens he used to steal motor cars by breaking in through the windows and then selling the cars. He did not know how to start a car, a stolen car, and you may think there was a certain amount of ridicule of him by the police, and rightly so. The police ended up with one of the officers saying that this was just a fairy tale.

Because he could not admit it, how the moneys came into his

account, because he would have to say yes, well, part of it comes from forecasting. So he invents this fantastic story.

Mr Calvert-Smith said to you in his final speech that Segers is, on his own admission, an accomplished liar. Hardly accomplished. You have only got to look at the nonsense that poured out of him, and the officers calling it a fairy tale at the end, to realize this is hardly accomplished.

As Hans Segers told you: 'I made it up.'

It is hardly a carefully constructed false account prepared beforehand, is it not? Hardly. He did not have to say anything at all.

He lied about Fashanu and the extent of his relationship with Fashanu and the telephone calls he had with Fashanu.

Why? It is obvious, is it not? Because where did he meet Lim and do his forecasting? At Fashanu's. Sometimes, as he told you, messages used to be left by Lim through Fashanu for Segers to get in touch with Lim. If he told you the truth about his whole relationship with Fashanu and how often he used to see him and how often he used to call him and how often he went to Fashanu's premises, the next question would be: 'Well, why did you go? What happened?' The forecasting would come out again.

My learned friend Mr Calvert-Smith made what, on the face of it, might have been a good point. Let us think about it for a little. He said this in his final speech: Why did not Mr Segers tell the police, when he was being interviewed, that he was in a property venture with Fashanu and a large sum of money had been given to him for the property venture?

That is nothing to do with forecasting, says my learned friend Mr Calvert-Smith.

You have only got to examine that remark made to you to realize that he could not say it, could he, because Mr Segers had already told the police he had no business with Mr Fashanu of any kind? He also told them, I never speak to the man. Having told the police that, how could he then go on to say to the police, Oh, this man I never speak to and had nothing to do with, by the way, we are in a business transaction in property.

140

I mean, once he had set course, the wrong course, and got on to that path, he could not get off it.

Members of the jury, he was a fool. Mr Segers was a fool, I suppose, not to have obtained the services of a solicitor before that interview.

He was probably a fool when you heard him admitting he had no precise idea how much he was owed by Mr Thuys.

He was probably a fool going along with a system in his ties business whereby he never received all the copy invoices from Holland with regard to the English orders that were placed.

Above all, ladies and gentlemen, he was probably a fool to lie to the police in the way in which he did.

As he said to you – and there is nothing else he could say to you – he said, I am sorry. I apologize. It was stupid, but he is not in the dock for being stupid. He is not in the dock for having made foolish decisions.

In our respectful submission to you, members of the jury, on a fair-minded assessment of the evidence, I ask you to find Hans Segers not guilty of this one charge he faces and to free him from the agony that has tormented him for two and a half years as the case has hung above his head, and to free him from the stain of the accusation that has been brought against him, so that he can resume his normal life at home and out there, giving pleasure to thousands and thousands of people who love football.

Deal with him as you will, but please, according to the evidence.

* * *

There were five powerful closing speeches, including David Calvert-Smith's, all of the highest quality, followed by the judge's summing-up. It is a fact of life that people pay most attention to the thing they heard last. David Calvert-Smith must have been well aware of this before going on first to be followed by the four defence counsel – although none of the defence teams were complaining. Calvert-Smith paid massive attention to detail, going through various charts to highlight his points, speaking in a very clear and eloquent manner.

Jerome Lynch, defending Lim, began in a witty and flamboyant style. He spoke in the language of the man of the street, addressing members of the jury using plain English at its best. He was theatrical to a point, drawing on his experience in working in the media on TV.

Trevor Burke had a totally different style. I believe that he appealed to one or two of the motherly females on the jury who felt some sympathy for him, especially after seeing him berated in the second trial by the learned judge on a matter of presentation. It was rather like a headmaster telling off a pupil. That kind of attitude can work against a judge if the jury have sympathy for the barrister, as I know they did in this case. In a way he had a harder task than others because his client, John Fashanu, exercised his legal right to silence, which gave the judge the right to tell the jury that an inference could be drawn from that. He needed to do quite a bit of explaining. He implied that successful and rich people, like his client, do not have to be dishonest. He adopted a 'prove it if you can' approach.

Rodney Klevan's closing speech, on behalf of Bruce Grobbelaar, focused on the character destruction of Chris Vincent, as it had to. There was no doubt that no one could have done that better. His choice of words, delivered with an underlying sense of humour and with a hint of a northern accent, could not be faulted. Apart from the judge, he was the senior lawyer at the trial, and his style oozed class and his character appealed to the jury. There is no doubt that a jury identifies with a lawyer and, if they do not like him, the client can suffer. The choice of lawyer is therefore of paramount importance.

The judge's summing-up was fair and factual, leading the jury through a minefield of information coupled with the usual remarks stressing that the prosecution had to prove their case beyond reasonable doubt. If the defence could show there was a measure of reasonable doubt, then the jury would have to acquit the four men in the dock. The defendants were then in the hands of the jurors.

It was an exciting and exhausting case and no one knew what

verdicts the jury would bring in. We studied them as they filed from the court after they had been given final instructions by the judge and tried to read any giveaway signs or feelings on their faces. They were all expressionless. Not one of them looked at the defendants and there was no hint of what their feelings might be.

We thought we had done enough to win, but probably the prosecution team felt the same way. I continued to be optimistic, as I had from the beginning, and I was sure that the jury would bring in the right result.

9

THE VERDICT

Waiting for the jury is always a nerve-racking experience, but at the second trial it seemed to take an eternity. The jury were sent out on the Friday and went home for the weekend. Then, twice a day, we were ushered back into the court to see if they reached a verdict.

When we were called back into court during the first trial, the announcement requested the presence in Court Three of all those involved in the Grobbelaar case. In the second trial it was officially known as the Lim case – all part of the Crown's attempt to minimize the risk of any effect on proceedings caused by the fame of those involved.

Every time we returned to Court Three we thought we would hear the verdict and our hearts were in our mouths. But instead of delivering a verdict, the jury would often enquire about certain circumstances concerning the case, or ask to see relevant video evidence again. On one occasion they asked to look at the scene involving Bruce Grobbelaar and Chris Vincent. They wanted to see if Bruce had picked up the sum of £2,000 or handed it back to Vincent, or put it in his pocket when leaving the room. There was some doubt about whether he took the money at all.

When one of the jury members complained about the quality of the sound, a typed transcript was provided. The prosecution had claimed that Vincent had refused to pick up an envelope containing the money, saying: 'No, no, no, you. That's yours.' But one jury member realized that it was actually Grobbelaar who was saying those words. The transcript had attributed it to the wrong person. So, after two and a half years of lawyers looking at all the documents and video evidence, it was a member of the jury who spotted this anomaly. Not surprising, really, when you consider that both men spoke with a Zimbabwean accent and both had apparently been drinking heavily.

The jury also picked up another important fact. Using equipment that improves the quality of the soundtrack, they detected Vincent asking Grobbelaar to carry a cash-filled envelope because the goal-keeper had a jacket and Vincent did not. These words did not appear in the transcript. I am sure those incidents were to play a major part in the decisions the jury finally arrived at.

Every day at about 4.20pm, we were asked to go back into court to hear if the jury had reached a verdict. When the jury were asked, 'Have you reached a verdict?' every day the same answer came back: 'No.'

But on the Thursday, 8 August, when they were asked the same question, after 26 hours and 20 minutes of deliberations over a period of five days, following 45 days of evidence, to our amazement, the jury foreman said: 'Yes.'

You could have cut the atmosphere with a knife. You could hear the defendants' wives on the balcony sighing with fear.

The jury foreman was asked: 'Have you reached a unanimous verdict on all the charges against Lim?'

The answer came back: 'Yes.'

'What is your verdict?'

'Not guilty.'

There were emotional screams from the balcony, and from Astrid

Segers in particular. If Lim had been convicted, our chances of success would have been that much smaller.

They then moved on to John Fashanu. The same question and the same answer: 'Not guilty.' By this time I could hear Astrid crying on the balcony. Melissa Fashanu was clapping.

Then it was Hans's turn. The jury were asked: 'Have you reached a unanimous verdict in the case of Hans Segers?'

'Yes.'

Once again my heart was in my mouth and I could hear Astrid on the balcony taking a deep breath and stifling a scream.

'What is your verdict?'

'Not guilty.'

Astrid screamed and burst into tears and Hans was discharged from the dock. Astrid ran down the stairs to hug him in the corridor outside.

Then it was Bruce's turn to face two verdicts. The first count was the same as the others: 'Not guilty.' But the jury had yet to make up their minds over the second charge, dealing with the sum of £2,000 from Chris Vincent. The jury had not made a unanimous verdict, nor even a majority verdict. So everybody was in the clear apart from Bruce, who had to come back the next day for the second verdict.

The two trials had cost the taxpayer a huge sum of money. The *Daily Mail* headline the next day was: 'The £15m cost of the fix that never was.' That summed it all up perfectly. It was not surprising that the police were bitter at twice failing to gain a conviction. But for the defendants, it was time to celebrate.

We rushed out of court to find Hans and Astrid hugging each other, both crying tears of joy and relief. I left them for a short time and then ushered them into a conference room so that they could have some privacy.

Then it was Jan's turn to burst into tears. Emotion was running high and, along with so many other people, I found it impossible not to shed a tear myself. I have never done that in court before or since.

Tears were streaming down everybody's faces and when

Desmond came into the conference room I even caught a glimpse of a tear in his eye, which I found remarkable, bearing in mind the famous courtroom battles he had been through. But this case, perhaps more than most, was full of human drama.

Everybody was hugging everyone else and Hans and Astrid hugged me, Jan, Stephen and Desmond. Astrid needed some urgent make-up repairs as her mascara had run all over her face.

Scoring the winning goal in a Cup Final or saving a penalty could have no comparison with these emotions. All the defence teams then embraced, although Bruce was still a little stony-faced as he was not over the last hurdle yet.

After some time Astrid finished crying and it was time for everybody to wipe away the tears. We emerged into the sunlight to face the barrage of flashbulbs and TV cameras. This time the sun shone brightly, unlike the weather which had greeted the result of the first trial earlier in the year, when everybody left the court in the pouring rain, uncertain as to what was going to happen next.

We made brief statements to the TV, radio and press, but Hans did not want to have a full press conference. David Hewitt had arranged a conference for Bruce, but Hans did not want to attend and I suspect that Bruce was not too keen, either.

We walked back through the town to the Wykeham Arms and the champagne flowed, bought by Desmond, as convivial as ever. The TV cameras joined us for some shots of us sipping our celebration champagne. It was difficult to describe the emotion of such an unbelievable day. All our hard work had paid off and we could all now begin to look forward. Desmond, in footballing terms, was the man of the match. He deserved most of the credit, because all of the defendants realized that because of lies Hans told in interview, the Crown saw Hans as the weak link in the defence chain, and that David Calvert-Smith would seek to destroy the defence case through him.

* * *

Hans takes up the story:

That final day was full of drama and one I will never forget for the rest of my life. During the rest of the trial there were times when your emotions swung like a pendulum. There were upbeat, positive days when you felt everything was going your way, and there were deep, dark, sombre, depressing days when the prosecution tried to hammer you into the ground.

It was a truly amazing feeling when the verdict finally arrived at the end of two trials and a nightmare passage of my life. The fact that the jury were finally ready to deliver their verdict took everybody by surprise. When we were called back into the court at 4.20 in the afternoon we were expecting to be told, as usual, to report back the following morning. But all of a sudden we were listening to the jury foreman announcing, 'Not guilty.'

When that verdict came, I stood up in the dock but my legs felt like jelly. They could hardly keep me upright. It was like doing 100 squats then being told to stand up. I know I've got big footballer's legs, but that day they really were quivering. At the same time Astrid was screaming with joy in the gallery and we couldn't believe that at last our ordeal was over.

* * *

The defendants all decided to return to court next day to support Bruce. They did not need to attend but stood by him in a spirit of fellowship. Only this time, instead of having to stand in the dock, they were able to watch proceedings from the visitors' gallery.

The judge, as ever, was anxious to stamp his authority on proceedings. He withdrew bail again and Bruce had to spend the morning in the court cells waiting for a verdict. I thought there was no legal reason at all for this kind of treatment. I thought it was petty in the extreme.

About three hours later, the jury came back and said they could not agree on a verdict. The judge directed that the jury be dismissed and the prosecution withdrew the charge.

This was equivalent to the charge being not proved rather than

Bruce being found not guilty, but nevertheless the result was the same. Bruce Grobbelaar had not been found guilty of anything and he emerged into the sunlight a free man. There were the hand-shakes, hugs and tears all over again. Bruce, as always, was immaculately dressed, sporting one of his famous fedoras. He made a brief press statement and then it was time for more champagne at the Wykeham Arms. I was so pleased for him and his loyal wife, Debbie.

News of the verdict was broadcast everywhere. As Jan and I drove back to London, my mobile phone never stopped ringing. After the umpteenth call, something inside it must have exploded and it never worked again.

The trial verdict featured prominently on television. I did a quick interview with Sky News going out at 7pm. Some people told me afterwards they thought I looked tired. That was not surprising. Later I drove home, showered and changed and did an appearance on BBC Newsnight at 10.30, by which time I felt a lot more relaxed and comfortable.

On Monday morning it was back to the office and time to catch up on eight months of work. It was also time for us all to start thinking about a holiday.

PART THREE

HANS BACK ON TRIAL

Enduring the agonies of the two trials at Winchester Crown Court was like a journey to hell and back for Hans Segers. The joy and relief of the not guilty verdict after the second trial meant he was free to resume his playing career. After being out of the game for almost two years, Hans was finally awarded a full-time contract by Wolverhampton Wanderers. But he still had another trial to face, as he prepared to face the full weight of the Football Association's disciplinary powers.

1

FACING THE FA

In December 1997, the Football Association charged Bruce Grob-belaar and me with breaching regulations concerning gambling on matches. At the time I was forecasting the results of Dutch matches, I was not aware of the FA rules concerning these matters. However, as they say, ignorance of the law is no excuse, so I pleaded guilty.

Having gone through the double trial at Winchester, this was another extremely nerve-racking period in my life as I wondered what verdict they would arrive at. My future was in the hands of the FA.

There were several options open to them. A small fine or a large fine. Or a small suspension or a long one.

The FA lined up with a QC and a solicitor to press their case. In court terms, it was like facing the police, prosecution and judge all over again. It was also like a Winchester reunion for the defence teams, as Bruce was represented by Andrew Eadis and I was defended by Jerome Lynch and Mel Goldberg with his assistant Jan Cook.

Bruce and I were charged with a breach of FA Rule 26a (iv), assisting with betting on any football matches other than authorized and registered football pools.

It was all down to how the FA chose to interpret the rules, and a couple of hours into the hearing I felt that we had no chance. There was no independent adjudication, but to have achieved that would have meant having the hearing in the High Court. That would have meant even more expense, and the trial had already cost me a fortune.

The FA imposed a fine and a ban, but both were suspended. That meant that Bruce and I could continue to play, and that was the main thing.

2

ON THE WEMBLEY TRAIL WITH WOLVES

A few months later, my career was given a terrific boost when I helped Wolves achieve a sensational victory away to Leeds United in the sixth round of the FA Cup. That victory came at the perfect time to put me in the shop window after twenty months out of the game because of the trial.

I had been on the bench for so long, both in the courtroom and as Wolves substitute, that I was getting desperate to play again. Luckily, I was called up to make my debut for Wolves in a midweek match at home to Stoke City on 4 March 1998, when the regular keeper Mike Stowell was injured. We were 1-0 up and should have killed it off, but in the second half Stoke had more of the play and grabbed an equalizer. At the end of the match we were booed off the field by the disgruntled Wolves fans, who had expected a team chasing a place in the promotion play-offs to beat a side fighting a desperate battle against relegation.

I made four good saves and must have played well enough to be retained in the side for the trip to Leeds on the Saturday, even though Mike was fit again. I felt nervous running out to play before a full house of almost 40,000 at Elland Road, but as soon as I saved the first shot, from Australian Harry Kewell, I knew that I was back. Kewell has a good left foot and knocked some great balls in for the strikers and the big guys known as the Leeds air-force. They certainly have some big, physical characters in that team. However, I am sure they took us for granted and underestimated us.

The match was fairly even right through and it was a real stale-mate until we took the lead with a superb goal from Don Goodman just eight minutes from the end. Then with two minutes remaining, Leeds were awarded a penalty, but I guessed the right way and saved from Jimmy Floyd Hasselbaink.

If that wasn't amazing enough, Hasselbaink then headbutted Keith Curle and as a Leeds attack broke down, I noticed that their goalkeeper, Nigel Martyn, had raced upfield to support their attack. Seeing him out of his goal, I took aim and tried to score from my own penalty area, but unfortunately I have to own up to the fact that I missed a sitter from ninety yards. That would have been an incredible goal, but I suppose the fairy story had to end somewhere!

At the final whistle, we raced to salute the Wolves fans who had been so vociferous, outshouting the home supporters in that huge Elland Road stadium. Those same fans had jeered us off the pitch on the Wednesday night. Now they were cheering us off the field on the Saturday afternoon following one of the greatest FA Cup upsets of recent years. Wolves fans are certainly hard to please, but once they are behind you there is no better following in the country.

After the match, the Wolves chairman Jonathan Hayward and his father Sir Jack, the president, accompanied managing director John Richards to the dressing-room to thank the players. I passed them in the corridor on my way to a TV interview. It was great to be back, and a wonderful feeling to see the headlines and pictures in the newspapers on the following Sunday and Monday.

Sky TV made me their player of the week and sent a camera

crew round to my house to do an interview. I only hoped that the publicity might help me land a new contract for the following season. Nothing had been discussed with me at Wolves, but I knew that the decision would have to wait until our promotion prospects had been decided. That is the key thing for Wolves. They have a fabulous stadium, good support, and everything is there in place for them to be a top club once again. They just need to get back into the Premiership.

What a week! First I make my Wolves debut on the Wednesday, it was our thirteenth wedding anniversary on the Friday, and on the Saturday this happens. It was just wonderful to be given my chance all over again and to show to everyone I could still do it at the top level. Saving the penalty was a fantastic feeling. It had been quite an ordinary game, but what an amazing finish.

I felt I had done my homework well on Hasselbaink. I had seen him take a few penalties before on television. Two he had placed low into the corner and one he had blasted over the top. As it was late in the game, I felt he was bound to go for the normal thing and try to place it again. Luckily, I guessed right. I had already made my mind up.

It seems every March throws up something amazing. Three years earlier in March came the big knock on the door by the police. The previous year in March we were waiting for the result of the first trial in Winchester. Now this. It doesn't get any better.

The following week I was in the headlines again for saving another penalty, this time in a 1-0 win over Crewe that kept alive our hopes of a place in the Division One promotion play-offs.

Two weeks later, on 5 April, I was back on the big stage again as Wolves faced Arsenal in the semi-final of the FA Cup at Villa Park. That match has to go down as one of the biggest games of my career. I was really pumped up and looking forward to it. Astrid brought the children up to watch and I got tickets for several members of my family who flew over from Holland. I also managed to get tickets for my co-authors Alan Thatcher and Mel Goldberg, who was torn between supporting me and his beloved Arsenal team.

Villa Park was full with nearly 40,000 people and most of the noise seemed to be coming from the Wolves fans. As we ran out on to the pitch we were greeted with a massive tickertape welcome and the fans let go thousands of black-and-gold balloons. That had been a feature of our FA Cup run. Wherever we had played, there were loads of balloons and lots of tickertape in the air as we came out. I remember the wind blew lots of the balloons towards the Arsenal end and there were so many of them that Tony Adams waved to the referee to hold up the kick-off while David Seaman and his defenders stamped on them in their goal-mouth. One of our guys joked that, even when he was bursting balloons, Nigel Winterburn could still only use his left foot.

It was wonderful for me to be involved in a match like that after what had gone on before. But I felt absolutely gutted that it was my miskick that led to them scoring after twelve minutes. On the day, most of my kicks were ending up deep in the Arsenal half. This one happened when I went to kick out an underhit backpass. I sliced it, but the ball still reached the halfway line. Steve Sedgley, one of our midfield players, was obviously expecting one of my big rocket launchers and he headed forward, no doubt thinking the ball would come sailing over his head towards the Arsenal penalty area.

Some of our other players also had their backs to our goal and didn't see the ball land at the feet of Patrick Vieira, who ran past a startled Steve and into space in front of our back four. Christopher Wreh was also finding some space out to my left and Vieira's accurate pass found him running free towards the goal. I came out to narrow the angle but he placed an inch-perfect shot beyond me as I dived to my right. It was a simple yet ruthless finish into the side netting.

Suddenly our supporters were subdued as the Arsenal fans found their voices. After that it was an uphill task getting back into the game. We battled hard and you could not have asked for any more from any of our players. They put up a tremendous battle, but at the end of the day it was eleven Nationwide League players up against eleven internationals from a top Premier League side.

Arsenal had won their previous four Premiership matches by a single goal, and here they were again in the same position. They are one of the best teams in the country at defending 1-0 leads, but it doesn't mean they are a negative side. They are a class outfit, and once they had scored we needed a bit of luck to get back into the game.

We had some good chances at the start of the second half – funnily enough, once when David Seaman dropped the ball only for it to skid away from Steve Claridge, who had joined us from Leicester City just before the transfer deadline. A similar thing happened soon afterwards when a shot ricocheted just beyond Steve's reach. Don Goodman battled away to try for a repeat of his goal at Elland Road, but the gaffer took him off twenty minutes from time and sent on Wolves legend Steve Bull. Despite Steve being a big Midlands star, this was the first time he had played at Villa Park, and the first time he had played in an FA Cup semi-final.

There were some tired legs and long faces at the end of the match. I walked off slowly and waved to the fans to thank them for their fantastic support. But I felt so sick inside that I just wanted to get back to the dressing-room. I was one of the first players to leave the pitch, as the rest of the squad went on a lap of honour. When the rest of the lads returned to the dressing-room, one of them gave me the shirt worn by my fellow Dutchman Marc Overmars. He had expressly requested that I should have it. What a wonderful gesture from one of Arsenal's real superstars.

It was such a shame that we were unable to score. We were so near, yet so far. The fans were disappointed, but not half as choked as we were. Having seen the goal replayed on TV, I know I sliced my kick, but the ball still reached the halfway line, so I don't think I was totally to blame. Certainly none of the players gave me a hard time over it. Someone was kind enough to say that it was my only mistake of the match.

I remember Don Howe, the former England coach, saying at Wimbledon that most players, if they are very lucky, might get the chance to play at Wembley once every ten years. You keep thinking that one day I'll get there, but maybe now I'm running out of years.

Watching Arsenal in the final, I was pleased that Overmars was the player who scored a magnificent goal to set Arsenal on the path to a 2-0 win over Newcastle and a famous Double triumph, their first since 1971 when my good friend Bob Wilson was in goal for them.

3

MY GREATEST SAVE

There have been some great saves in the history of football. Gordon Banks's save against Brazil in the 1970 World Cup is one that will always be remembered, along with the Dave Beasant penalty save for Wimbledon in the FA Cup final against Liverpool in 1988. I even have some memorable ones of my own, like the penalty save for Wolves against Leeds in the FA Cup sixth round which meant we went into the semi-final. But my greatest save was when the Lord saved me.

On my passport, under religion it said RK, which stands for Roman Catholic in Dutch. My parents are both Catholic, but we never went to church unless it was for a wedding or a funeral. I remember at Astrid's father's funeral I made a joke about the priest's strange clothes. I thought he looked like a magician, the kind you see in some cartoons. I suppose on reflection that was a little disrespectful, but that was my attitude to church and God.

I had some big questions about life, like we all do. Why are there air disasters and murders and illnesses? The big question for me was, is there life after death? I was concerned about these things but I never thought for a moment that God might have the answers; in fact, if the truth be known, I really blamed God for all these things. If He was a God of Love and all-powerful, why did He let these things happen? And as for the church, it was full of sad people. It was definitely not for me.

But I was wrong. My marriage had been going through some big problems. Like most men, I was not really aware of how bad it was, but looking back now I can see that Astrid, my wife, was at her wits' end. I was in great danger of losing her and my two children, whom I really love. Astrid's sister, Petra, who is a Christian, along with Adrie, her husband, who is a Baptist Minister in Belgium, had been encouraging Astrid and talking to her about the Lord Jesus and how He could help our marriage.

I didn't go along with this, but Astrid started to go to church with some friends. After a short time, she became a Christian and started to read the Bible. I didn't understand at first what was happening and wasn't really too happy about it, so much so that Astrid would cover her Bible to make it look like another book so that I didn't know what she was reading.

Astrid started to change. It was small things at first, but she was definitely different. Although our relationship wasn't getting any better, she was happier in herself. Radiant is the best way to describe it. I knew the change was nothing to do with me, but it was so remarkable that I really had to take notice. We talked about it and Astrid said that it was because the Lord had given her a new start and she really wished that I could become a Christian, because then I too could have a new start – and the way things were going, that was the only way our marriage could be saved.

It was a very emotional time. I realized then that the biggest change in Astrid was that she was willing to forgive me, and I finally understood how close we had come to her packing her bags and leaving me. I knew she was right. My life, although successful from a football point of view, was privately in a real mess. You can only be Jack the Lad for so long. I knew that I had to change, I didn't want to lose my family – but I didn't know what to do.

We got into the car and drove to Belgium to speak to Petra and Adrie. They explained things so simply. They said that God had sent Jesus so that we could have all the wrong things we have done, what the Bible calls sins, forgiven. They told us that when we trust in Jesus and ask Him into our hearts, He gives us a new life and wipes the slate clean so that we can start afresh.

I could see that this had clearly happened for Astrid and I wanted this too. So right there and then, I asked the Lord Jesus to come into my heart. I said sorry to Him for all the wrong things I had done, for how I had hurt Astrid and my family, and asked Him to forgive me and give me this new life. I had never really prayed before, so I wasn't too sure what to expect. But what happened was amazing. I felt such great relief. The Bible talks about the peace of God. I didn't know what that was because I had never read the Bible before, but now I know because that is what I had, for the first time in my life.

That peace has never left me, even throughout all the ordeal of the court cases. That's not to say that I have never been worried since, or that life became a bed of roses. In fact, the reality is that my personal circumstances obviously got worse. But I can honestly say that God has never left me since the day I asked Jesus into my heart. I have made mistakes and still do, but the Bible says that 'if we confess our sin, He (Jesus) is faithful to forgive us our sins.' Jesus is pure and holy and He wants us to be like Him. One mistake I made was to lie to the police when I was arrested. It was a stupid thing to do and got me into big trouble. I'm sorry for that now, not only because it cost me a lot in terms of the pain my family went through at the time, but because it was wrong and I let God down. But even through that He was faithful. I think He knew that I was just a new Christian and I was frightened. Even though I had messed up again, He helped me through it.

But I've jumped on a bit. When we got back home from Adrie's, it felt like I was in a daze. Everything was so different, so new. My love for Astrid was new, it was like we were on honeymoon again.

I'm not normally what you might call a sensitive man, but even I could tell I was different. I started to go to church with Astrid and soon found out that Christians are not 'sad people' at all, but people who are warm and friendly. They didn't want to know me just because I was famous, or a football star. I found that status doesn't matter to real Christians. They were interested in me as a person, and this was really refreshing. I want to say at this stage that some people think that when you become a Christian, that that is the end of fun. That is definitely not true. I like to have fun, and that was all part and parcel of the Crazy Gang era at Wimbledon.

Christianity is fun, Christians are fun, the Church is fun. Our church has modern music and a real family attitude. I joined what is called an Alpha Group, learning about God and His Son Jesus and what it means to be a Christian. There I discovered the answers to those questions I had. I learnt that God really is a God of Love. It is because He loves us so much that He gives us freedom of choice. Many of the bad things that happen are not because of God, but because of man, because he has decided not to follow God. We conveniently blame Him because it diverts attention from the truth, that we are the ones who are wrong and that we are really very selfish. The amazing thing is that God hates the wrong things we do, but He really loves us.

The best thing for me, though, was to learn that there is life after death. I was really afraid of dying. In the Alpha Group I discovered that when I became a Christian, I received a free gift. The Bible says that 'God so loved the world that He gave his only Son, that whoever believes in Him might not perish but have eternal life.'

God did this so that we can be saved. When we die, if we believe in Jesus, we go to Heaven. This isn't fantasy, or magic. It is reality. It's back to the choices bit – Heaven or Hell, we choose. These places are real, and our destination depends on the choices we make now. This was a real bonus for me. I had made the right decision. Jesus had saved me, given me a new life, and replaced my fears of death with hope for an eternal future in Heaven with

Him. My greatest save! We felt nothing could destroy our happiness now.

It's hard to describe what happened next. The police knocked on the door and suddenly we were swept into a nightmare. I still sit and wonder about it all. To be honest, it all happened so quickly that I forgot about God. But I am so glad, though, that He did not forget about me.

By the time I had come to my senses, I had already failed Him and my family. I was confused and panicking and I thought that if I just said anything it would all go away. I was really very foolish, but what followed next still amazes me. God showed up in a big way. A lot of people assumed that I was guilty. Even people I thought were friends assumed that what the papers said was true. It's at times like these that you find out who your real friends are. It was also at this time that I discovered that the people who I had previously thought 'sad' were, in actual fact, very special people.

They took me at my word. They came round and prayed with me and encouraged me. They took care of my family. Throughout that time many people came up to me and said, 'We know that you are a Christian and we are praying for you.' This was also a great encouragement to me. It was at this time that I discovered that God speaks to us. It's not voices in your head. We've all heard about these murderers who claim they kill because God told them to. It's not like that. My Christian friends would ring up or come round with a passage from the Bible that they said God wanted to encourage us with. Time and time again these passages spoke directly about our circumstances. This was no hit-and-miss thing. God was clearly saying, 'I will never leave you or forsake you,' and He was proving it.

One particular passage came from the Old Testament. It says, ' . . . we have no power to face this vast army that is attacking us. We do not know what to do, but our eyes are on you.' That was exactly how we felt, but the passage goes on with God's response: ' . . . You will not have to fight this battle alone. Take up your positions; stand firm and see the deliverance the Lord will give you. Do not be afraid; do not be discouraged. Go out to face them tomorrow, and the Lord will be with you.' You may think, so what, that doesn't mean much – except that this passage was given to me the day before I took the stand in the second trial. Throughout the whole time I was on the stand, that passage was a constant strength and reminder that the Lord was with me.

More than that, God kept His word. He continually answered our prayers. One occasion always brings a smile to my face. Before the closing speeches, we had prayed that Mr Calvert-Smith, the prosecutor, would not say anything with clever words that would confuse or mislead the jury. When he got up to speak, his microphone was not working properly and nobody noticed, or didn't want to tell him, till after lunch. This meant that a good part of his summing-up was unheard. The judge asked the jury if they wanted to hear it again, and they said no thank you. God has a sense of humour.

When the second trial came to an end, and I was acquitted, I just thanked the Lord. I could not have made it through without Him. There is an account in Exodus, Chapter 17 where Joshua was fighting the Amalekites. Moses was praying and when he held his hands up, Joshua was winning. When Moses's hands dropped because he was tired, the fight went the other way. As Moses became tired, two of his friends held his hands up so that he was steady, and Joshua won the battle. When we keep praising God, like Moses was, God helps us win life's battles.

In my case, my friends and family helped me to keep my hands up and God saw me through. There is one passage of God's word that is very special to me. It's special because of its relevance throughout the trials and also because it is for all of my life. The Book of Proverbs says: 'Trust in the Lord with all your heart and lean not on your own understanding; in all your ways acknowledge him, and he will make your paths straight.'

When I became a Christian I had no idea that I would have to go through all of this. When I look back, I can say that if I hadn't been a Christian I could not have coped, and who knows where I would be now? I have no doubts in God or in Jesus, His Son. He has proved his love for me over and over again. Life as a Christian is at times difficult. Every decision you make, you have to ask yourself: is this what Jesus would do?

When you look around the world you can see sin and evil everywhere, but Jesus is pure and lived without sin. He is a hard act to follow, but I have decided to follow Him and can prove that when we trust in Jesus, He does make our paths straight. The Bible says that when we become a Christian, 'we are a new creation; the old has gone, the new has come.'

Sometimes it's good to let the past go; in fact, it's vital if we are to move forward. As a Christian, every day is a bonus, every day is a new adventure, with new people to meet and share with. Life is about sharing. God is about sharing. Some people are worried about the future, that's why they cling on to the past so much. But Jesus said, 'Do not worry about tomorrow.' Because of what He has done in my past, I know I can trust Him for the future. Jesus never lets us down. Whether it's football, business or anything else He may call me to, I'm thankful to Him and look forward to each day that He sends. I can't wait to meet Him and thank him for what He's done for my life.

As for the future, naturally I want to keep on playing for as long as I can, but coaching is another possibility. I have had a goal-keeping school with Phil Parkes for several years, but finding the time to develop it has always been a problem. Ideally, I would like to work for a major club and be responsible for coaching the goalkeepers and be involved in youth development. I worked as a coach with Bob Wilson and have also been to America to coach goalkeepers. I would like to help my best mate, Graham Smith, to develop his business with the contacts I have built up over the years. His company instals burglar alarms and smoke detectors. Working overseas is another possibility and so the start of another adventure may be just around the corner. England has been an adventure. But I believe the Lord will put me where He wants me, either in a job or the country I will live in.

In hindsight, I suppose in one sense I regret the day I met Richard Lim. That meeting certainly changed my life. But the experience of the trials, and my faith in God, has made me a much stronger person.

POSTSCRIPT

THE FUTURE

Hans Segers was released by Wolverhampton Wanderers at the end of the 1997–8 season. His ambition was to secure another contract with a major club, combining coaching with playing. Newspaper speculation linked him with a move back to PSV Eindhoven, where Bobby Robson had returned as coach after a successful spell with Barcelona. On 29 July 1998 Hans signed for Tottenham Hotspur, as reserve goalkeeper behind Ian Walker and Espen Baardsen. He also joined the legendary Pat Jennings on the White Hart Lane coaching staff, with responsibility for coaching the goalkeepers. David Pleat, the Tottenham Director of Football, had seen Hans on television giving a sermon during a religious service in Paris at the beginning of the World Cup. He later telephoned Hans to see if he was available. The contractual negotiations were handled by Mel Goldberg.

Bruce Grobbelaar is coaching Zimbabwe and hoping for a contract to continue playing in England. He is considering launching a libel action against *The Sun*.

John Fashanu is working as a sports promoter-manager and is advising boxer Herbie Hide. He is also a United Nations sports ambassador.

Richard Lim is planning to launch a new business.

Chris Vincent is believed to have returned to South Africa. Charges against him of attempting to pervert the course of justice were dismissed. He had spent almost a year in prison on remand.